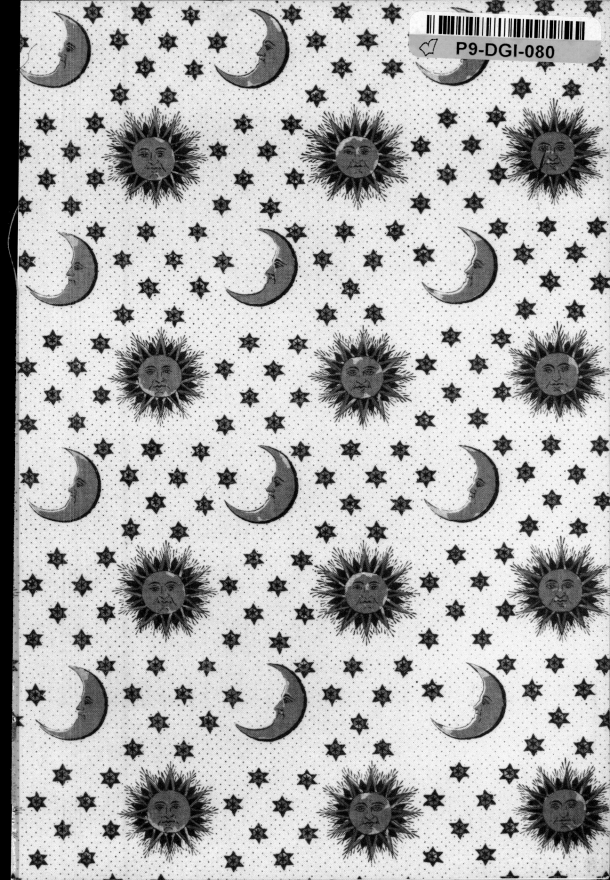

FABRICS

FOR HISTORIC BUILDINGS

A Guide to Selecting Reproduction Fabrics

J A N E   C .   N Y L A N D E R

The Preservation Press

The Preservation Press
National Trust for Historic Preservation
1785 Massachusetts Avenue, N.W.
Washington, D.C. 20036

The National Trust for Historic Preservation is the only private, non-profit national organization chartered by Congress to encourage public participation in the preservation of sites, buildings and objects significant in American history and culture. Support is provided by membership dues, endowment funds, contributions and grants from federal agencies, including the U.S. Department of the Interior, under provisions of the National Historic Preservation Act of 1966. For information about membership, write to the Trust at the above address.

Third edition
Printed in the United States of America
87   86   84   83   5   4   3   2   1

Library of Congress Cataloging in Publication Data

Nylander, Jane C., 1938-
    Fabrics for historic buildings.

    Bibliography: p.
    1. Textile fabrics — Reproduction.   2. Historic buildings — Conservation and restoration.   I. Title.
TS1767.N94   1983   747′.5   83-9798
ISBN 0-89133-109-3

Jane C. Nylander is curator of textiles and ceramics, Old Sturbridge Village, Sturbridge, Mass.

The Preservation Press gratefully acknowledges the assistance of Scalamandré in the production of the cover.

Cover: LODDON, 1884. Designed by William Morris. Scalamandré. (See page 116.)
Endleaves: SUN, MOON AND STARS GLAZED CHINTZ, c.1790—1820. Brunschwig and Fils. (See page 55.)
Pages 6—7: ST. CYR, c.1790—1810. Brunschwig and Fils. (See page 67.)
Pages 18—19: CASHEMIRE COTTON, 1865. Brunschwig and Fils. (See page 91.)

CONTENTS

INTRODUCTION

FABRICS FOR HISTORIC BUILDINGS

F abric furnishings — curtains, upholstery, bed hangings, table covers and incidental ornamental fabrics — are a fundamental part of the restoration or period interpretation of any historic building. The visual impact of a room is largely dependent on the design and color of the textiles used within it, and the impression of a particular historical period depends on the accurancy with which these textiles are selected and installed. Because textiles are highly perishable and because they were changed more frequently than architectural details, few original fabrics are available for use. Carefully selected modern reproductions are often the most authentic fabrics available.

This book is intended to help people with limited fabric experience select and order documentary reproduction fabrics as well as other kinds of fabrics that are suitable for furnishing historic properties. While the book addresses basic historical, curatorial and practical considerations, it is not intended as a substitute for the careful study of period documents, secondary sources and reproduction fabrics themselves.

The catalog sections of this book list reproductions of fabrics used in the United States between 1650 and 1900. They are organized by period and fabric type. Brief discussions of the characteristic fabric furnishing styles of each period are provided as a general guide to the evolution of fabric design, changes in textile technology and popular styles of drapery and upholstery. These discussions should be supplemented by works cited in the bibliography and by specific research related to the restoration or furnishing problem at hand. A glossary is included as a general aid that could be expanded through additional reading and research.

The catalog entries provide specific information for selecting and ordering commercial reproduction fabrics. Where it was not possible to illustrate designs, references to illustrations in other published sources have been given. The companies listed are highly regarded for the quality of their products. Fabric companies change their offerings as often as once or twice a year, introducing new designs, retaining successful patterns and discontinuing those that do not sell well or present production difficulties. As a result, the reader should keep in mind that some fabrics listed in this book may be discontinued and that new and appropriate, but

An example of restoration work in which currently available fabrics (Brunschwig and Fils's "Bird and Thistle Toile" and "Coralito") were selected to approximate the visual effect, color and date of the original documented set of bed hangings. The John Brown House, Providence.

unlisted, patterns may be introduced. Fortunately, some manufacturers keep the printing screens and weaving patterns of discontinued styles, and in such cases it may be possible to obtain a discontinued design through special order.

The fabrics reproduced commercially today are more an indication of their present popularity than a reflection of their popularity in their original periods. The years following 1920 saw an increasing use of silk damask and brocade in "traditional" 18th-century designs; in less formal interiors, reproductions of copperplate-printed textiles called "toiles" were popular, and the bold two-color resist prints had an especially strong appeal. Period rooms in museums as well as traditional interiors in private homes made abundant use of these types of fabric. Many accurate reproductions of period textiles were commissioned for specific restoration projects, but the fact that they have remained commercially viable reflects their present popularity. As a result, some fabrics that were rare in 18th-century America, such as woven silks and resist prints, are now reproduced in great quantities, while the more commonly used woolen textiles are seldom reproduced.

This situation is changing to reflect new trends in historic house restoration and popular taste. The new interest in accurate and well-documented interior restoration has resulted in the careful reproduction of more of the common period textiles. A much greater variety of reproductions of 18th-century wools can now be found, and more are being planned. Many newly reproduced designs reflect the growing interest in late 19th-century design and Victorian chintzes. Fabrics must be chosen carefully, however. The ready availability of William Morris designs today does not necessarily mean that they were the first choice of average late 19th-century Americans, any more than rich silk damasks were found in the houses of average Americans during the colonial period.

WHY USE REPRODUCTIONS?

Why should fabric reproductions be considered for use if original fabric is available? Period designs usually call for so much yardage that the use of antique textiles would be impossible. In those rare cases where original curtains or ample original yardage has survived, preservation of the original materials should be the primary goal. In most cases these original fabrics have survived only because they have been carefully protected from light, dirt and insects; exposure would only hasten their destruction. Virtually no circumstances justify the damage caused to original textiles by exposure to light and dust for long periods.

Displaying certain antique textile items such as quilts or other bed coverings may be acceptable on a short-term basis, provided the light in the room can be controlled. If original objects cannot be rotated regularly, a reproduction should be substituted for everyday display. In no case should original objects be left out for long periods.

The practice of cutting up original bed curtains, bedspreads, quilts, coverlets and other artifacts for curtains or upholstery also should be avoided. Such uses are historically inaccurate as well as destructive. Even cutting up old linen sheets for use as curtains or the base of embroideries is unacceptable. This practice is also impractical: The weakened fibers will not survive long, and the new work will be lost as well.

The use of reproduction fabrics, therefore, allows the preservation of original documents while recreating authentic period effects. An additional benefit of using reproductions is that the fabrics can be cleaned by modern commerical methods and can be replaced when necessary to maintain the freshness of the colors and appearance.

A documentary reproduction fabric is a modern textile that copies as accurately as possible a historic original, or document. In some cases fabrics that are not specifically termed documentary reproductions are also suitable for restoration work. Some mid- or late 19th-century designs have never been discontinued. In addition, plain-woven fabrics of pure fibers, which have changed little over time, are still available from a variety of commercial sources. Machine technology has produced some alterations in width and texture, but by and large these changes are acceptable. The catalog sections of this book cite some specific examples and sources of nondocumentary fabrics appropriate for historic buildings, but these are only suggestions.

DOCUMENTARY RESEARCH BEFORE FABRIC SELECTION

A common mistake in restoration is to neglect preliminary documentary research and instead arbitrarily select a date for restoration (often the date of original construction of the building) and then look for beautiful designs and materials appropriate to that date. Some of the interiors created by this procedure would probably astonish the original owners, who might never have dreamed of having silk draperies made from designs published in Paris the year they were married.

Few projects will have the documentary evidence and surviving material to ensure accurate restoration to a single early date. The selection of a broad time frame, on the other hand, opens up a considerable range of choices. For example, what style of curtain is appropriate for an 18th-century house in which most of the furniture dates from the mid-19th century and which was inhabited by the same family from the time it was built up to the early 1900s? Or what does one do with an otherwise Federal-style interior if original curtains survive from the 1870s? What if the room's function has changed? The choice of appropriate furnishings grows out of a comprehensive understanding of the property and its occupants, one that expands rather than limits the impression of the whole.

The first task in selecting fabrics for use in historic interiors is to establish the purpose of the restoration or rehabilitation and the extent and quality of existing documentation. The adequacy of documentary evidence may, in fact, determine whether the restoration is to emphasize an exact date or a broad historical period. If samples of original textile material (or written descriptions of colors and fabrics, early photographs or even drawings) have survived, then consider whether it is desirable to recreate a specific moment in the history of a particular room or building. If so, the search for commercially available reproductions that approximate the surviving documents can begin. Now is the time also to consider ordering custom reproductions.

If, on the other hand, no evidence exists about the use of earlier furnishing textiles, what does one do? The first step is to undertake research in primary sources specifically related to the house and to similar houses in the same geographic area. These sources include inventories, diaries, letters, account books, photographs, paintings, newspapers, design books, advice books and magazines. It is important to know as much as possible about the interior before making any decisions. Ask these kinds of questions: How old is the building? Who built it? What purpose did it serve? How was each room used? If the building is a house, how many people lived there? How old were they? Were they married? If so, when? How many children did they have? How long did their descendants live there? Was this their first house? When was it remodeled and why? What was the owners' economic status within the community? Did they purchase furnishings locally? If not, did they order them from a commercial supplier? Did they travel? If so, where? What might they have seen? In other words, what sources of fabric and design were available to the owners within their known geographic and economic limitations? The answers to such questions will guide the researcher in gathering information and making decisions.

With the intent of the restoration determined and the historical research carefully done, decisions can then be made about the period to be represented. Because the furnishing fabrics will be a major factor in recreating a period effect, the importance of selecting the fabrics and using them in proper context cannot be overemphasized. If possible, study original textiles from the selected period before choosing a reproduction fabric. Becoming familiar with the appearance of original textiles also provides a better basis for judging the accuracy of reproduction work. Many major art museums and historical societies maintain textile study collections that can be viewed by appointment. A good source for locating collections in a particular geographic area or with a given speciality is Cecil Lubell's three-volume guide *Textile Collections of the World*.

If it is not possible to examine original textiles firsthand, one should at least study details of design and printing illustrated in published sources. Probably the most helpful books are Florence Montgomery's *Printed Textiles*, the Victoria and Albert Museum's *English Printed Textiles: Large Picture Book No. 13* and Clouzot and Morris's *Printed and Painted Fabrics*. Detailed photographs of original fabrics can be ordered from textile study collections. There is no substitute for seeing the original example, however; details and texture cannot be conveyed accurately by photograph, and lens distortion may be misleading.

SELECTING REPRODUCTION FABRICS

The choice of a reproduction fabric should be guided by the results of historical research. However, one should understand that, no matter how expensive or how carefully supervised, fabric produced by modern methods will not exactly duplicate the original appearance of its historic counterpart and that exact duplication is not always the primary goal. In addition, each project will have specific economic and technical requirements that must be considered. Before attempting to choose from the fairly large selection of documentary reproduction fabrics currently on the market, it is crucial to define the variations of the original that are acceptable for the given project.

One might assume that the fiber must always be the same — that silk originals should be reproduced in silk, wool in wool, cotton in cotton. The possibility of using synthetic yarns, however, is likely to arise when the costs of silk or wool are considered and the durability of synthetics is compared with that of natural fibers. "Victoria Damask" (page 105) is a modern reproduction in rayon, cotton and wool that achieves substantially the texture of the original wool drapery fabric. "Chateau sur Mer" (page 103) is a printed version of an original silk brocade with excellent visual fidelity to the document. Persons responsible for a restoration will have to decide whether they can afford the most technically accurate reproduction possible or whether a reasonably exact duplication of visual effect is the goal.

The current appeal of the "country" look has resulted in a large number of fabrics based on original period textiles but changed slightly so that they cannot be considered true reproductions. Handwoven coverlet designs have been printed on cotton. Embroidered and stenciled motifs from original pieces have been transposed onto printed fabric with little regard for the integrity of the original piece of which they were a part. Pieced and appliqued quilts have similarly been used as design sources with individual motifs carefully copied and repeated in yardage ad infinitum. Since none of these original designs was intended to be used in endless repeats, they cannot be considered appropriate for restoration projects in which the goal is the accurate reproduction of the original visual effect.

In choosing a reproduction fabric, one should be aware of differences caused by the changing technology of textile production during the past 200 years. In no case can modern commercial spinning and weaving processes duplicate the appearance or texture of hand-production methods, nor can chemical dyes exactly duplicate the colors achieved by vegetable dyes. The silk-screen and steel-roller printing and the photoengraving methods often used for reproductions cannot exactly duplicate the visual effects of the original block or copperplate printing or of hand engraving. Some reproductions using these methods do remarkably well, but inevitably some detail is lost.

The standard loom sizes also have changed; modern warps are longer and, thus, widths are greater than those of earlier periods. In some cases the original designs can be printed or woven double to fit the wider cloth, but more often they must be adjusted slightly in order to produce a unified design. Sometimes large copperplate designs cannot be reworked into modern widths; in those cases, the original design may be reproduced with large unprinted areas at the sides. Damask designs may be reduced vertically by half, using only one of the original motifs.

The texture of goods selected for printing or of yarns for woven designs is crucial to the success of a reproduction. Be aware that the original document has probably lost body through wear and cleaning. On the other hand, if too coarse a texture is selected for printed designs, design detail will be lost. Slubs, or lumps on threads, which in the past were regarded as undesirable imperfections in spinning, should not be arbitrarily added to modern goods in an attempt to make them look old. Similarly, reproduction of faded color or background discoloration, known as "aged grounds," does a disservice to a design that was printed originally on white cotton or linen.

The use of undocumented colors is inappropriate in authentic restorations. In most commercial reproduction fabrics, the color of the original is reproduced and designated the document color, such as "document blue" or "documentary colorway." Most commercial reproductions are available in nondocumentary colors as well, in which case the original color is often listed as *1* in the catalog code number series for that fabric. One or two of the other available colors may have been possible historically, but in most cases the modern colors were unknown in the past and could not have been created with the dye technology then in use. An accurate restoration project must be designed within the framework of the technology of the restoration period, no matter how repetitious or strange it may seem.

Sometimes an acceptable reproduction is entirely inappropriate for use as a furnishing fabric because the document would not have originally been used that way. Some accurately reproduced clothing fabrics are currently available, but because they are not suitable for restoration work, they have not been listed in this book. In rare cases, such a fabric might be used for a slipcover or a bed covering. Reproduction clothing fabrics are excellent, of course, for reproducing a pieced quilt. "Country Linen" is a modern clothing fabric based on an American 18th-century handwoven linen grain sack. In addition to the documentary natural fibers, it is available in several colors and described as "a modern fabric with traditional texture and quality." This attractive fabric is used today for a variety of decorative effects, but in the 18th century grain sacks probably were never used for furnishing fabrics. Always be sure that the reproduction fabric could have been used in the restoration context intended.

When writing to a manufacturer to request a catalog, be sure to specify that the fabric sought is for restoration purposes. Some manufacturers will provide loan samples for restoration projects on request, and samples are also sometimes available through local interior designers. Before contacting a manufacturer, it is advisable to (1) assemble all data and photographs pertinent to the restoration, as well as any available original fabrics, and (2) complete preliminary restoration plans, including specific requirements, such as the period to be recreated, the full measurements of all surfaces to be covered, the planned use of the room and the projected work schedule. When placing an order, be sure to check accuracy of number, colorway, width and repeat. If the fabric is to be used for drapery or bed hangings, give the length and number of cuts in case the manufacturer finds it necessary to supply goods in more than one piece. If you require delivery in one piece, be sure to specify that on your original order. When ordering a fabric not currently in stock, be sure to ask how long the delivery time will be. It might be wise to add at least two or three weeks to your own planning schedule beyond the time quoted by the manufacturer; sometimes delays will be even greater.

When ordering goods, be sure to request a current run cutting, which is a sample of the color currently available, in order to ensure that it is the same color as the sample originally approved. At this time specify the amount of yardage needed. It may be possible to reserve that amount of fabric for 10 days while approving a sample, thus speeding up the order time and avoiding the possibility that available goods will be sold out while the cutting is approved. Check the cutting also for the quality of printing; worn-out screens produce heavy blots of color that are not desirable. When ordering handblocked goods, expect color variation even within one piece. When an order is received, examine the entire yardage for any flaws that would make it unacceptable.

CUSTOM REPRODUCTION WORK

When seeking the most exact reproduction possible of a specific prototype fabric, a client usually has to arrange for the custom manufacture of a limited amount of yardage and the accompanying trimmings. (It is also possible and somewhat less expensive to obtain special color runs of currently available designs.) A frequent illusion of historic house restoration committees with cherished samples of original fabric is that by offering a sample to a company for inclusion in its commercial line, the company will in turn provide all the fabric for the restoration project as well as pay a handsome royalty. Occasionally, a manufacturer can be persuaded to include a special design as part of the regular commercial line, paying a royalty at stated intervals. In such cases, the costs to the client are considerably less, but this situation rarely occurs. One should approach custom work with the clear-eyed expectation that it will be very expensive and that the company is really doing one a favor to work to exacting specifications.

In custom work, the client usually must bear the expenses of setting up the looms or cutting the printing screens and of reproducing the original color and design as well as the expenses of materials and labor. The price may vary depending on the yardage required, small amounts of yardage being the most expensive. In most cases, a 50 percent deposit is required. Negotiation for custom reproduction work is inevitably a highly personal experience. Among the few companies willing to undertake custom work on a limited basis are Brunschwig and Fils, Clarence House, Lee Jofa, Old World Weavers, Scalamandré and Schumacher. All are experienced in working with museums and can be commended for their cooperative attitude and excellent workmanship.

Signing a contract and paying a deposit are only the first steps in a long process. For a company to finish a custom-woven or custom-printed product can sometimes take 16 to 18 months. It is wise to check on the work at every step of production, approving actual samples and color strikeoffs. Modern production methods and dyestuffs are not the same as those used to produce the original, so do not assume that the reproduction will be flawless. The client has the right to insist on as perfect a reproduction as possible, with full understanding and approval of any changes made by the company. Because of delays in the expected delivery time and other reasons, there may be increased charges, so determine in advance whether the price estimate represents a maximum charge or whether allowance should be made for inflationary cost increases. Be sure to have firm price estimates in hand when seeking funds and to allot a percentage of the budget for possible cost overruns.

The manufacturer may recommend that a certain percentage of additional goods be ordered at the outset to compensate for possible flaws. No manufacturer will make adjustments for imperfections once goods have been cut, so it is imperative to examine the entire yardage when it is first received.

CONSTRUCTION AND INSTALLATION

Once the reproduction fabrics have been chosen, a number of questions remain. When actually making up the goods, decide on the degree of accuracy to which the reproduction furnishing must adhere. If an original curtain or bedspread was hand-stitched, unlined and perhaps fastened with iron tacks, should the modern reproduction be machine sewn, lined and fastened with Velcro? In making such decisions, keep in mind the original purpose of the restoration. If the major goal is a decorative effect, by all means choose the best modern construction and installation methods. The fabrics will last longer and be much easier to clean. If, on the other hand, the goal is the interpretation of a way of life at a given moment, the completed work should be as faithful to the original as possible. To achieve this, all stitching should be a close approximation of the size and type of handwork or machine work done on original examples. Lining should be used only if there is a prototype.

Original hanging methods should be duplicated if at all possible. If design motifs are not matched where widths are joined or if designs have been used upside down or sideways, these details should be carefully reproduced. Indeed, matching horizontal repeats in work for periods before 1840 or 1850 is seldom necessary, because it seems not to have been a standard practice at that time. When such practical details cannot be determined from an original example, careful study of existing documents and published designs and illustrations from the period may be necessary.

HOW TO USE THE CATALOG

The following catalog of fabrics suitable for use in historic buildings is divided into two parts. The first section presents documentary reproduction fabrics and is arranged by historical period. The second part, "Modern Textiles: Continuing a Tradition," lists nondocumentary and plain-woven fabrics and is arranged by type of fabric.

Individual catalog entries give the following information when it is available:

Manufacturer's catalog name for the fabric pattern
Country, date and method of manufacture of the original
Source of a published photograph of the document fabric (see
    bibliography for complete titles)
Fiber content of the reproduction fabric
Width of the reproduction fabric and repeat (length of one com-
    plete pattern motif)
Design changes made by the manufacturer in the reproduction
Organization or museum for which the fabric was reproduced
Information about the document and its location
Manufacturer's catalog number for the reproduction fabric
Manufacturer's name for the document color. (The word "series"
    following a catalog number means that the fabric is available in
    more than one color and that the manufacturer has not specified
    the document color. Some of the colors available may not be of
    the period; "alternate color" indicates colors appropriate for the
    period.)
Addresses of fabric manufacturers are given on pages 141–42.

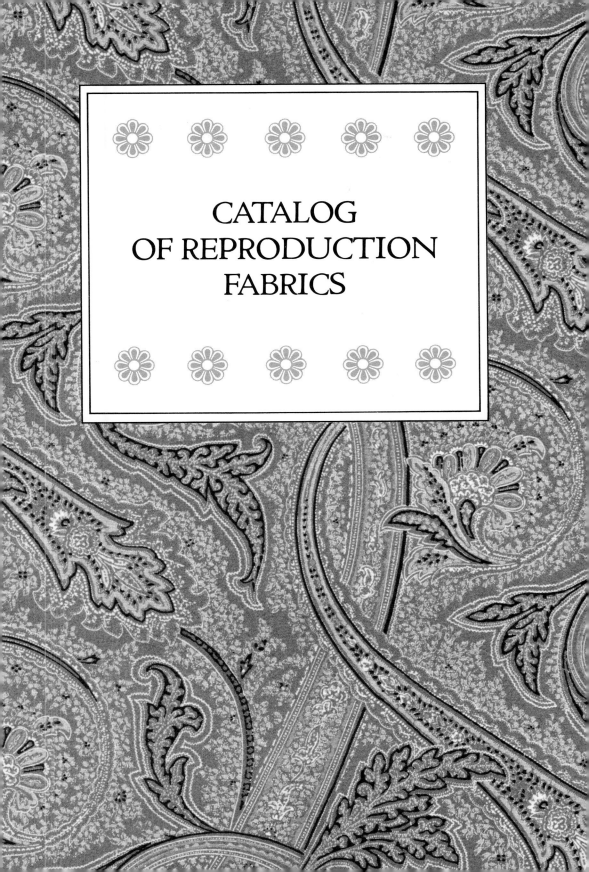

CATALOG
OF REPRODUCTION
FABRICS

1700 TO 1790:
A PREFERENCE
FOR IMPORTED FABRICS

Throughout the 18th century, Americans preferred imported fabrics for furnishing their buildings. English fabrics predominated because they were protected by high tariffs imposed by the mother country on goods imported into the colonies from other countries. Indian goods also were imported under the protective arm of the British East India Company. The quality of fabrics made for export varied, but for the most part these goods were far superior to anything made in colonial America. Although some households produced woolen and linen goods for their own use and some professional weavers and a few linen stampers were able to make a living, throughout the colonial period domestic textiles usually were made for clothing.

The 18th century saw the beginnings of industrialization in textile manufacturing in England, but the new technology was a closely guarded secret that did not reach this continent until the end of the century. Not until the removal of trade restrictions (a result of American independence) and the establishment of American textile mills were goods made here in any quantity. Even then, British and, to some extent, French fabrics were favored for their superior quality, design and color.

Brilliantly colored and highly finished wools were among the most sought-after imports for both clothing and household furnishings. These were tightly spun, highly finished fabrics with a hard, crisp surface, totally unlike most modern wools. Silks were used primarily for clothing, although a few wealthy merchants, plantation owners and royal governors made use of silk draperies in their best chambers or parlors.

Colorful printed textiles were the primary vehicles by which all sorts of pictorial designs reached average Americans. Throughout the period, designs were handprinted from cumbersome woodblocks, the colors developed through a complex series of steps. In the middle of the century, the introduction of direct printing from engraved copperplates on cotton or linen greatly expanded production and made possible the fine linear designs with large repeats that were especially well suited for use in household furnishing.

In both woodblock and copperplate printing, the colors were primarily deep indigo blues and the rich purples, reds and pinks derived from

TURF INN TOILE PRINT, c.1780–95. Lee Jofa. Blue or sepia.

21

madder. Many of the madder colors have faded to sepia or brown tones as a result of extensive exposure to the sun. In studying an antique fabric document to determine the original color, examine it carefully for areas that have been protected from the sun. A tiny space inside a seam or under a thread or border tape may preserve a surprisingly bright coloration. Details that appear to have been printed in brown may, in fact, have originally been purple.

In some 18th-century textiles, additional colors were "pencilled" or added with woodblocks to the monochromatic copperplate designs. As dye technology evolved, new colors were possible. It was not until 1814, however, that a good green could be printed directly on cloth. Before that time, green required a two-step process in which blue was printed over an area previously printed yellow. If such a print was out of register, blue and yellow showed at the edges of all green areas. Frequently the yellow dyes were not as permanent as the blue, and as they faded, the green areas became blue. Many floral printed textiles that now appear to have been printed with blue stems and leaves were originally printed in green, but because of the fugitive nature of the yellow dye they now appear blue. Reproductions of such fabrics should duplicate the original green, but unfortunately they often do not.

Typical 18th-century block-printed fabric designs include large-scale flowers and birds on open white grounds, a style derived from imported Indian chintzes. After the middle of the century, delicate rococo scrolls and shells and some chinoiseries were added to the design vocabulary of textile printers. Large-scale arborescent designs, with their endless stems and handsome birds and flowers, predominated in the 1780s. During this period, fine dotted work was added to accentuate individual motifs or to fill in the entire background.

Fabric printing from engraved copperplates was invented by Francis Nixon at Drumcondra, Ireland, in 1752. By 1756 he had moved his operation to Surrey, England, where the technique was soon adopted by other textile printers. Their designs included pastoral and classical landscapes, chinoiseries, rococo scrolls, birds, literary and theatrical subjects and commemorative designs. Some of these designs derived from contemporary prints; others were specially commissioned for textile printing.

The large scale of the plate-printed designs made them especially suitable for household furnishings, particularly for bed hangings and counterpanes. As early as 1761, the *Boston Gazette* carried an advertisement for "Cotton Copper Plate Furniture for Beds." Many examples of American bed hangings made of these fabrics have survived and should be studied in detail by those who wish to reproduce them. Such details as width of fabric, matching or mismatching of motifs, thread, size and type of stitches, trimmings and evidence of original hanging methods should all be noted in addition to the shape of the valances and style of curtains. A good example of a reproduction bed of this period is that at the John Brown House, Providence, R.I. (page 8).

By the late 1770s copperplate printing began to be developed in France, especially by C. P. Oberkampf at Jouy. His work reached such a level of quality that the term "toiles de Jouy," meaning cottons printed in Jouy, has become almost a generic term for copperplate-printed textiles. For many years the fact that this style of printing had originated in England was not known, and both French and English designs were referred to as "toiles." After the American Revolution, some French plate-printed fabrics were imported into the United States and used as furnishing fabrics. These designs received a renewed interest at the end of the 19th century. For that reason many of the plate-printed textiles listed here are also suitable for restoration work at later periods, but they are listed only once, at the time of their introduction.

People recreating colonial interiors have available a tempting yet misleading choice of fabrics. Many excellent reproductions of 18th-century silks, linens and printed cottons are available today, but there is little evidence to support their use in 18th-century American buildings. For example, "Rivière Enchantée" is an excellent reproduction of a beautiful early 18th-century Indian textile reflecting Javanese influence, but it is doubtful that it was ever imported into colonial America. A less obvious problem is that created by the many silk damask designs that have been used so lavishly in "Georgian" interiors of the last quarter century. They are good reproductions, but few of them were used in 18th-century America.

For those rare cases where site-specific research indicates the use of handwoven domestic wool or linen fabric, a custom reproduction can be made fairly easily by a skilled weaver. Some specialists are included in the list of suppliers (pages 142 – 43), but many others can successfully accomplish this work. Take care to approve the threads selected and be sure to obtain a woven trial to ensure that the color and texture are close to that of the fabric to be reproduced. (See Constance Dann Gallagher's *Linen Heirlooms* and *More Linen Heirlooms*, J. R. Bronson's *The Domestic Manufacturer's Assistant* and, for natural dyes of the period, Rita Adrosko's *Natural Dyes and Home Dyeing*.)

Documentary evidence shows clearly that in the colonial period few houses were embellished with elaborate bed and window hangings or softly upholstered furniture. Many people slept in pallet beds placed directly on the floor in rooms shared with children, cooking equipment, tools and storage containers. Statistical analysis of probate inventories, such as those published by Susan Schoelwer and Abbott Lowell Cummings, or of upholsterers' account books, such as that published by Brock Jobe, makes clear that even in such seemingly spartan interiors, imported textiles and the work of professional upholsterers played an important role in providing a modicum of comfort. Obviously these same textiles provided color and design in spaces where there was little of either.

For those who could afford domestic luxury during colonial times, the most lavish use of fabrics was in the covering and hanging of the best bed.

In many probate inventories, the value of beds with hangings far exceeds that of any other piece of furniture in the house. Bed hangings of woolen stuffs, such as harrateen, cheyney or moreen, were popular from the beginning of the century. Green was the most common color, with crimson and scarlet the next most popular colors. In the early 1700s, white linen was sometimes used for hangings, and soon colorful calicos and dramatic blue-and-white checks became more common. Copperplate-printed cottons were used during the last 40 years of the century, but wool continued to predominate, at least in the Mid-Atlantic states and New England. Because of the work involved in their construction, embroidered, or "worked," curtains were rare.

Some bed hangings were imported ready-made from London, but patterns for the latest designs also were imported by urban upholsterers and quickly copied. The typical shapes of bed valances changed several times throughout the 18th century, but the basic formula continued to be tester cloth, head cloth, valances and bases, all of which were nailed to the bed frame, and movable head and foot curtains, the latter usually twice the width of the former. Often the scrolls of the valances were outlined with decorative border tapes or strips of fabric used as borderings, but the remaining pieces might be plain. Often the selvages at the sides of bed curtains were not even hemmed.

Some bed chambers had window hangings of the same fabric and style as those of the bed hangings. The most luxurious had upholstered furniture to match. For example, the "Yellow Chamber" of the Moffatt-Ladd House (1764), Portsmouth, N.H., was furnished before 1768 with bed and window hangings of yellow silk and wool damask in the "half drapery" style. Eight side chairs, an easy chair and three window-seat cushions were also covered in this fabric (see Cummings, *Bed Hangings,* fig. 12). The wallpaper of this room had a yellow background as well. Color coordination was clearly important in the 18th-century interior.

Eighteenth-century window hangings were probably even more rare than fully hung beds. A committee or curator charged with the accurate restoration of a room interior of this period should be prepared to find that the room might not require window curtains, even if 20th-century taste seems to require them. Fortunately, when restoring a period house or creating a period interior for private living, it is not necessary to recreate the original room; selection of appropriate reproduction fabrics and the use of period upholstery techniques will produce quite satisfactory results.

In the 18th century a curtain was defined as a piece of cloth that could be expanded or contracted at pleasure to admit or exclude light or air. Its purpose was considered functional rather than purely decorative. For that reason, few curtains of this period were fixed at the perimeters of the window frame. Until the invention in the 1790s of French rod curtains, which permitted curtain panels to be pulled apart horizontally, several systems of opening and closing curtains were employed. The curtains could be drawn up vertically in a style known as Venetian curtains (the mechanism is exactly that of Venetian blinds), or they could be pulled up diagonally by cords threaded through rings and pulleys, resulting in the graceful swags of the "festoon" or "drapery" style. Such curtains could be made with single panels at each window (half drapery) or with two panels; they could be drawn up in single or double drapery, depending on whether one or two cords were used in each panel of fabric.

Bed or window curtains could be threaded on wire, string or iron rods; they could also be nailed to the bed or window frame or to a wooden lath that projected above the window at any height deemed suitable. The curtain panels could fall to the sill, to the floor or almost anywhere in between. If threaded on a wire or rod, curtains were usually made with a tiny casing at the upper edge. Sometimes, window curtains were made with tiny tape loops (one-half inch or less) at the upper edge; bed curtains usually were made with longer loops, probably to make them easier to open from a prone position.

Recent careful analysis of surviving 18th-century furniture with its original upholstery has revealed much about upholstering techniques and the finished appearance of the work. Written sources have shown that the most common cover for chair seats that did not match bed or window hangings was black leather, rather than the colorful silk damasks used on this style of furniture in the mid-20th century. One common practice of 18th-century craftsmen was to define the outlines of their work with rows of bright brass tacks or decorative tapes. Because of the type of stuffing and this use of tacks and tape, the furniture of this period had a taut outline, in contrast to the soft contours of modern spring seats and foam rubber padding.

Expensive fabric covers for seating furniture were often protected by loose cases or slipcovers of printed or checked cotton, dimity or linen. These cases were probably used most of the time, being removed only for the most important social occasions. Correctly made reproductions may appear sloppy to the modern eye, for the name "loose cases" aptly described their fit. Not only were they loose and wrinkled in appearance, they also were often attached with visible tapes or strings, tied together in floppy bowknots. The lower edges of the cases were often finished with a ruffle, sometimes extending to within a few inches of the floor.

Few original examples of 18th-century curtains or cases have survived, and it would certainly be a mistake for every restoration to make slavish copies of these few. Rather, the originals should be carefully studied for their construction techniques and sewing details, which should be used to guide the cut and construction of appropriate fabric furnishings. The important point is not to use 20th-century techniques for this work. Pinch pleats and flannelette interlinings, wide loops or ties of double thicknesses of matching fabric, bias piping and skin-tight slipcovers were unknown in the 18th century. For accurate restoration work, it is as important to use appropriate construction techniques as it is to select the appropriate fabric.

HAMBLEDON WOOL
DAMASK, c. 1750–1830.
Brunschwig and Fils.
Document vermilion.

WOOLS

BRUNSCHWIG AND FILS

❋ HAMBLEDON WOOL DAMASK. English, c. 1750–1830. 46% wool, 54% cotton. 50″ wide, 19¾″ repeat. Documents at Brooklyn Museum, Winterthur Museum and Maryland Historical Society. Original is a worsted woolen furnishing fabric with an embossed design intended to imitate damask; this fabric is an adaptation in which the design motifs have been actually woven as a damask. No. 60311.01 (document vermilion). Alternate colors: No. 60313.01 (saffron); No. 60314.01 (wintergreen); No. 60312.01 (indigo).

❋ MOREEN WOOL TEXTURE. Probably English, 18th or 19th century. 100% wool. 48″ wide (no center fold). Reproduced for Metropolitan Museum of Art and Museum of Early Southern Decorative Arts. No. 38693.01 (document gold); No. 38696.01 (document coral). Available plain or with moire design.

❋ VERPLANCK DAMASK. English or Flemish, probably late 18th century. 100% wool. 19½″ wide, 59″ repeat. Reproduced for Metropolitan Museum of Art, used in the Verplanck Room in the American Wing. No. 60293.01 (document gold). Alternate colors: No. 60294.01 (green); No. 60291.01 (red).

SCALAMANDRÉ

❋ CREOLE MOIRE'D MOREEN. Probably English, 18th or early 19th century. 40% linen, 60% wool. 50″ wide. No. 1946-3 (yellow).

❋ EARLY AMERICANA MOREEN. French, c. 1760–1835. 25% linen, 50% wool, 17% cotton, 8% silk. 51″ wide. Document at Schuyler Mansion, Albany, N.Y. No. 1945-1 (old red strié, embossed); No. 1945-2 (old red strié, not embossed).

❋ INDEPENDENCE HALL BAIZE CLOTH. English, 18th or early 19th century. 100% wool. 50″ wide. Document at Independence National Historical Park, Philadelphia. No. 99243-1 (green).

VERPLANCK DAMASK,
late 18th century.
Brunschwig and Fils.
Document gold.

KANDAHAR PRINT,
KANDAHAR BORDER,
mid-18th century.
Brunschwig and Fils.
Multi on cream.

BIRD AND THISTLE,
c. 1790. Brunschwig and
Fils. Red.

HAMPTON RESIST,
1740–80. Brunschwig and
Fils. Blue.

HOMAGE D'AMERIQUE
TOILE, c. 1786.
Brunschwig and Fils. Red
on white.

❀ MASSACHUSETTS TAFFETA MOREEN. English, c. 1750–1825. 100% wool. 48″ wide. Document privately owned. No. 99459-1 (bottle green).

❀ MILITARY TWILL TEXTURE. English, c. 1670–1790. 90% wool, 10% nylon. 51″ wide. Worsted document privately owned; reproduces texture and streaky dyes of original. No. 99301-10 (rust); No. 99301-8 (gold); No. 99301-4 (green); No. 99301-2 (navy). Minimum order for special colors 200 yards.

❀ NEW ENGLAND DAMASK. English, c. 1760–80. 100% wool. 49¾″ wide, 44″ repeat. Document on easy chair owned by New England Historic and Genealogical Society, Boston. No. 97385-1 (gold).

❀ XVII CENTURY ANTIQUE DAMASK. English, c. 1750–1800. 100% wool. 50″ wide, 34″ repeat. From a silk document. No. 90022-11 (red); No. 90022-12 (gold); No. 90022-14 (olive green).

SHUMACHER
COLONIAL WILLIAMSBURG REPRODUCTIONS

❀ PEYTON RANDOLPH DAMASK. English, c. 1775–1800. 100% wool. 52″ wide, 23″ repeat. Document at Colonial Williamsburg. No. 32910 series.

❀ WILLIAMSBURG WOOL. English. 100% worsted wool. 54″ wide. Adapted from background of an 18th-century worsted damask. Document at Colonial Williamsburg. No. 86055 (spruce).

❀ WILLIAMSBURG WOOL SATIN. English, c. 1725–1825. 100% wool (two-ply worsted). 52″ wide. Document at Colonial Williamsburg. No. 82690 series.

STROHEIM AND ROMANN

❀ CUMBERLAND. English, c. 1750–1800, woven damask. 100% cotton. 50″ wide, 25″ repeat. Adapted from original woolen damask in textile collection of Winterthur Museum. No. 39810-39817 (red—original color).

PRINTS

BAILEY AND GRIFFIN

❀ BIRD AND BOUGH. English, c. 1770–90, block print. 100% cotton. 48″ wide, 38½″ repeat. Document privately owned. No. 03475 (red and green on cream).

BRUNSCHWIG AND FILS

❀ BALLON DE GONESSE. French (Jouy), 1784–85, copperplate print. Clouzot, pl. 14; d'Allemagne, pl. 135. 100% cotton. 39″ wide, 38½″ repeat. Document at Cooper-Hewitt Museum. No. 37251.01 (red).

❀ BIRD AND THISTLE. English, c. 1790, copperplate print. 100% cotton. 54″ wide, 32″ repeat. Documents at Winterthur Museum and Brunschwig Archives. No. 65751.01 (red).

❀ BROMELIA RESIST. English, c. 1765, resist-dyed cotton with border design. Montgomery, *Printed Textiles,* fig. 192. 100% cotton. 44" wide plus 2½" border on each side, 29" repeat. Document a quilt at Winterthur Museum. No. 76862.04 (indigo).

❁ CANTON RESIST. English or American, c. 1750–70, resist dyed. 100% cotton. 54" wide, 28½" repeat. Document in Textile Study Room, Metropolitan Museum of Art. No. 73052.04 (indigo).

❁ CHINOISERIE TREE. English, c. 1750–70, block print. 100% linen. 54" wide, 65" repeat. Document at Winterthur Museum. No. 72371.01 (crimson).

❁ COMTESSE DE MAILLY COTTON PRINT. French, mid- to late 18th century, block print. 100% cotton. 54" wide, 21" repeat. Document privately owned in France. No. 173610.00 (madder colors with blue on white ground).

❁ CREIL COTTON PRINT. Indian, mid- to late 18th century, block printed and painted on cotton. 100% cotton. 50" wide, 48" repeat. Document privately owned in France. No. 171300.00 (madder colors with blue on cream ground).

❁ DEBORAH LOGAN. Indian, mid- to late 18th century, block print. 100% cotton. 48" wide, 10¼" repeat. Document a quilt found at Stenton, home of James and Deborah Logan, Philadelphia. No. 73422.04 (indigo on off-white).

❁ DURAS PAINTED TAFFETAS. Chinese export, probably 18th century. 100% silk. 48" wide, 25½" repeat. Document in Textile Study Room, Metropolitan Museum of Art. No. 39130.00 (multi on cream).

❁ GRAND GENOIS PANNEAU. Indian, mid-18th century, printed and painted palampore for European market. 100% cotton. 63" wide, 91" repeat (cut by panel only). Document privately owned. No. 173490.00 (multi on white).

❁ HAMPTON RESIST. English, c. 1740–80, resist print. 56% cotton, 44% linen. 46" wide plus 2" border on one side, 34" repeat. Document at Winterthur Museum. No. 77312.04 (blue).

❁ HOMAGE D'AMERIQUE TOILE. French (Jouy), c. 1786, copperplate print designed by Jean Baptiste Huet. Clouzot, p. 25; d'Allemagne, pl. 144. 100% cotton. 39" wide, 37¾" repeat. Document in Brunschwig Archives. No. 37421.01 (red on white).

❁ KANDAHAR PRINT, KANDAHAR BORDER. French, mid-18th century, madder and indigo block print. 100% cotton. Print 31" wide, 54¾" repeat; border 15½" wide, 31½" repeat. Document owned by manufacturer, Oberkampf, Alsace, France. Print No. 172300.00, Border No. 172310.00 (both multi on cream).

❁ KANDIA COTTON PRINT. Indian, mid-18th century, block-printed and painted cotton. 100% cotton. 61" wide, 12¼" repeat. Adaptation; based on motifs in Indian block-printed piece. Document privately owned in France. No. 65951.01 (red).

❁ LA FORÊT IMAGINAIRE. Western Indian, late 17th century, painted and dyed cotton. 100% cotton. Panel 51" wide, 116" repeat (cut by panel only). Also available as adaptation, without printed base of panel, 50″ wide, 90″ repeat (cut by repeat only). Document from Ashburnham House, Sussex, England; now at Cooper-Hewitt Museum. Panel No. 174242.00, Yardage No. 174252.00 (both blue and brown on cream).

❋ LA VALETTE. Indian, early 18th century, printed and painted cotton for the European market. 100% cotton. 40″ wide, 13½″ repeat. Document privately owned. No. 172750.00 (multi on cream).

❋ L'EVENTAIL. French (Jouy), c. 1785, block print. 100% cotton. 50″ wide, 5″ repeat. Document privately owned. No. 173224.00 (green).

❋ MANSARD COTTON PRINT. Indian, mid-18th century, block-printed and painted cotton. 100% cotton. 50″ wide, 21″ repeat. Yardage based on motifs in a printed and painted panel with borders on four sides. Document privately owned. No. 174400.00 (multi).

❋ MIRANDE. French, c. 1785–90, block print. 100% cotton. 48″ wide, 16″ repeat. Document privately owned. No. 37510.01 (cream ground).

❋ NEPAL. Indian, late 18th century, madder and indigo painted cotton. 100% cotton. 55″ wide, 19¼″ repeat. Document privately owned. No. 173661.00 (red and blue on cream).

❋ PANNEAU INDIEN. Indian, mid-18th century, printed and painted cotton. 100% cotton. 56″ wide, 85″ repeat (cut by repeat only). Hand-blocked. Document privately owned in France. No. 170530.00 (cream ground).

❋ PEONY TREE. English, c. 1780, block print. Montgomery, *Printed Textiles*, fig. 81. 100% cotton. 54″ wide, 36″ repeat. Document owned by Winterthur Museum. No. 73231.04 (madder and indigo).

❋ PETITS CHAMPS COTTON PRINT. French, c. 1775–1800, block print. 100% cotton. 50½″ wide, 31¼″ repeat. Document owned by Winterthur Museum. No. 73581.04 (red and blue on cream).

❋ PHILADELPHIA STRIPE. American (Philadelphia), 1775 or 1776, block print. Montgomery, *Printed Textiles*, fig. 164. 100% linen. 50″ wide including 2″ overmatch, 9¼″ repeat. Design by Walters and Bedwell; the earliest identified signed product of an American textile printer. Document owned by Winterthur Museum. No. 73811.04 (red and cream).

❋ PRANCING DEER. English, c. 1750–80, resist print. 56% cotton, 44% linen. 46″ wide plus 2″ border on one side, 32½″ repeat. Document a quilt at Winterthur Museum. No. 77332.04 (blue).

❋ RIVIÈRE ENCHANTÉE. Indian, early 18th century, block print showing Javanese influence. D'Allemagne, pls. 213 and 213B. 100% cotton. 49½″ wide, 29″ repeat. Document privately owned in France. No. 174151.00 (red).

❋ SAUMUR COTTON PRINT. French, mid-18th century, block print. 100% cotton. 50″ wide, 17½″ repeat. Document privately owned in France. No. 173891.00 (red and blue).

❋ SHERWOOD. French (probably Oberkampf), c. 1780, block print. 100% cotton. 52½″ wide, 5″ repeat. Document a privately owned paper design for a textile. No. 172910.00 (multi on cream).

❋ SIKAR. Indian, mid-18th century, hand painted. 100% cotton. 50″ wide, 20″ repeat. Document privately owned. No. 172910.00 (multi on cream).

❋ SRINAGAR. Indian, mid-18th century, hand painted. 100% cotton. Yardage adapted from a panel with borders; 31″ wide, 27½″ half-drop repeat. Border 11″ wide printed with three strips on 33″-wide fabric, 30″ repeat. Document privately owned. Yardage No. 172700.00, Border No. 172710.00 (both multi on cream).

❋ TOILE D'INDE. Indian, mid-18th century, block print, probably for the English market. 100% cotton. 48″ wide, 18¾″ repeat. Reproduced for Museum of Early Southern Decorative Arts. Document at Metropolitan Museum of Art. No. 75400.04 (red and green).

❋ TOILE DUPLEIX. Indian, late 18th century, madder and indigo block print, probably for the European market. 100% cotton. 51″ wide, 46″ repeat. Document at Victoria and Albert Museum. No. 173640.00 (multi on white).

❋ VILLANDRY. French (Jouy), c. 1785, block print. 50% linen, 50% cotton. 50″ wide, 38″ repeat. Document in Brunschwig Archives. No. 172272.00 (blue).

❋ VILLEFRANCHE. French, c. 1785, resist dyed. 45% cotton, 55% linen. 48″ wide, 26½″ repeat. Document in Brunschwig Archives. No. 75292.04 (blue on white).

❋ VILLEROY PRINT ON LINEN. French (Jouy), c. 1785, block print. 56% cotton, 44% linen. 48″ wide, 12½″ repeat. Document the lining of 18th-century quilt made of Indian palampore, found in France; owned by the Cooper-Hewitt Museum. No. 73930.04 (red and blue on cream ground).

CLARENCE HOUSE

❋ BUCKS COUNTY. Swiss-German, 18th century, resist print. 60% linen, 40% cotton. 52″ wide, field repeat 3¼″ with border repeat 12″. Traditional design. No. 32041-3 (blau).

❋ CORNE D'ABONDANCE. India, 18th century, block-printed and painted palampore. 100% cotton. 63″ wide, 20″ repeat. Handblocked. Document privately owned. No. 31762-1 (multi on bise).

❋ DEERFIELD. Swiss-German, 18th century, resist print. 60% linen, 40% cotton. 51″ wide, 12½″ repeat. Traditional design. No. 32042-3 (blau).

❋ L'ARBRE FLEURI. French, c. 1750–1800, block print. 100% cotton. 60″ wide, 43″ repeat. Document privately owned. No. 31854-1 (blanc).

❋ LES PAMPRES. French, late 18th century, block print. 100% cotton. 50″ wide, 17½″ repeat. Document privately owned. No. 31783-1 (white).

❋ RAYURE CORNE D'ABONDANCE. Indian, 18th century, block-printed and painted palampore. 100% cotton. 63″ wide, including a 20″ border stripe, 27″ repeat. Handblocked. Document privately owned. No. 31763-1 (multi on bise).

PEONY TREE, c. 1780.
Brunschwig and Fils.
Madder and indigo.

SHERWOOD, c. 1780.
Brunschwig and Fils.
Multi on cream.

top left
RESIST PRINT, c.1776.
Scalamandré. Blue.

top right
FRENCH RESIST,
c.1770–80. Scalamandré.
White and blue.

left
PHILIPSBURG MANOR
RESIST, c. 1750–75.
Schumacher. Indigo blue.

DECORATORS WALK

❁ AMERICAN INDEPENDENCE. English, c. 1783–1800, copperplate print. Montgomery, *Printed Textiles,* fig. 300 ("Apotheosis of Benjamin Franklin and George Washington"); d'Allemagne, pl. 131. 100% linen. 48″ wide, 28¼″ repeat. Document in many textile collections, usually printed on cotton. No. L65057 (plum); No. L65059 (brown).

GREEFF FABRICS

❁ PLEASANT BAY. English, c. 1760–80, resist print. 100% cotton. 56″ wide, 28¼″ repeat. Screen-printed with printed ground simulating quilting. Document at Shelburne Museum, Shelburne, Vt. No. 61355 (ink blue).

❁ SHALIMAR. English, late 18th century, block print. 100% cotton. 56″ wide, 3½″ repeat. Document privately owned in England. No. 60400 (rose and gray blue on sand).

LEE JOFA

❁ AVIARY TOILE PRINT. English, c. 1780–95, copperplate print. 100% cotton. 36″ wide, 32″ repeat. Document privately owned. No. 298050 (rose and ivory); No. 298052 (blue and ivory).

❁ PEONY PRINT. English, c. 1780, block print. 100% cotton, glazed. 47″ wide, 34½″ half-drop repeat. Recently converted from handblocked print to rotary screen. No. 799600 (multi).

❁ POMEGRANATE PRINT. English, c. 1770–80, block print. 100% cotton, glazed. 50″ wide, 30″ repeat. Document privately owned. No. 637080 (antique white).

❁ TURF INN TOILE PRINT. English, c. 1780–95, copperplate print. Montgomery, *Printed Textiles,* fig. 270; Victoria and Albert Museum, *English Printed Textiles,* fig. 158. 100% cotton. 54″ wide, 30″ half-drop repeat. No. 729073 (blue); No. 729074 (sepia).

SCALAMANDRÉ

❁ DON QUIXOTE TOILE. French (Nantes), c. 1785, copperplate print. D'Allemagne, pl. 160. 100% cotton. 34″ wide, 38½″ repeat. Document owned by Scalamandré. No. 6445-1 (wine on beige).

❁ FLOWER BASKET. English, c. 1770–80, resist print. Montgomery, *Printed Textiles,* fig. 189. 100% linen. 50″ wide, 17½″ repeat. Adapted from document at Metropolitan Museum of Art. No. 6412-2 (blues on ecru).

❁ FRENCH RESIST. French, mid-18th century, resist print. 44% linen, 56% cotton. 48″ wide, 22″ repeat. Screen-printed adaptation from document in textile collection of Metropolitan Museum of Art. No. 6410-1 (indigo on natural).

❁ FRENCH RESIST. French, c. 1770–80, resist print. 100% cotton. 54″ wide, 27″ repeat. Document privately owned. No. 7735-1 (white and blue).

❀ ITALIAN COUNTRYSIDE. Drumcondra, Ireland, 1752–57, copperplate print. 100% cotton. 51″ wide, 35¼″ repeat. Design attributed to Francis Nixon; first successful copperplate printing of textiles. No. 7588-3 (red on off-white).

❀ PAISLEY. English, c. 1770, resist print. 100% cotton, glazed. 38″ wide, 13½″ repeat. Document privately owned. No. 6216-11 (blue and white on dark blue).

❀ RESIST PRINT. English, c. 1776, resist print. Montgomery, *Printed Textiles,* fig. 191 ("Pheasants"). 100% linen. 46¼″ wide, 26″ repeat. Document at Metropolitan Museum of Art. No. 6218-1 (blue).

❀ RODNEY. English, c. 1770–80, block print. 100% cotton. 36″ wide, 34½″ repeat. Document owned by Scalamandré. No. 6236-1 (red, blue and brown on tan).

❀ TREE OF LIFE PANEL. India (Coromandel Coast), c. 1775–1800, block-printed and hand-painted cotton. 100% cotton. 45¼″ wide, 109⅞″ repeat (cut by panel only). Document is window drapery owned by Kenmore, Fredericksburg, Va. No. 6728-1 (multi on white). Sold by the pair. For special orders, length or width of panels can be adjusted.

❀ WASHINGTON-FRANKLIN TOILE. English, c. 1783–1800, copperplate print. Montgomery, *Printed Textiles,* fig. 300 ("Apotheosis of Benjamin Franklin and George Washington"); d'Allemagne, pl. 131. 100% cotton. 33″ wide, 33½″ repeat. Document in many textile collections. No. 6012-11 (light red on cream).

SCHUMACHER

❀ KHYBER. Indian, 18th century, block print. 100% cotton. 54″ wide, 27⅝″ repeat. Document in Schumacher Collection. No. 73460 (woodrose).

❀ PHILIPSBURG MANOR RESIST. English or American, c. 1750–75, resist print. 58% linen, 42% cotton. 54″ wide, 31″ repeat. Document at Sleepy Hollow Restorations, Tarrytown, N.Y. No. 65555 (indigo blue). Special order only.

❀ VAN CORTLANDT HONEY COMB FLORAL. English, c. 1760–80, block print. 66% linen, 34% cotton. 54″ wide, 19″ repeat. Document at Sleepy Hollow Restorations, Tarrytown, N.Y. No. 65514 (blue).

❀ WARREN TOILE. French or English, c. 1780–90, copperplate print. 100% cotton. 50″ wide, 35″ repeat. Document owned by Preservation Society of Newport County, Newport, R.I. No. 161322 (brick).

SCHUMACHER
COLONIAL WILLIAMSBURG REPRODUCTIONS

Unless otherwise cited, all documents are in the textile collection of Colonial Williamsburg, Williamsburg, Va.

❀ BANYAN PRINT. Indian, c. 1775–1800, block print. 100% cotton. 54″ wide, 18″ repeat. Document a man's dressing gown. No. 73790 (document red and blue).

WASHINGTON-
FRANKLIN TOILE,
c. 1783—1800.
Scalamandré. Light red on
cream.

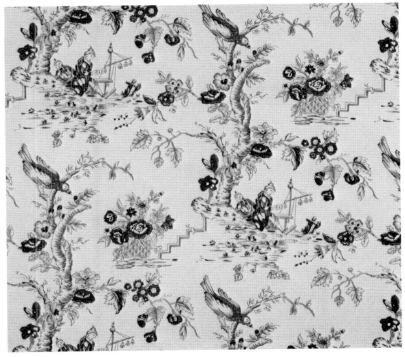

top left
BOTANICAL CHINTZ,
c. 1765–1800.
Schumacher. Document
red and green.

top right
CALICO BIRD, c. 1780–90.
Schumacher. Document
red.

left
CHINESE BELLS,
c. 1770–80. Schumacher.
Document red.

JARDIN CHINOIS,
c. 1760—80. Schumacher.
Document blue and red.

❋ BOTANICAL CHINTZ. French, c. 1765—1800, block print. 100% cotton. 54″ wide, 26¾″ repeat. No. 72990 (document red and green).

❋ BRUTON RESIST. French, c. 1740—1800, resist print. 100% linen. 54″ wide, 13″ repeat. No. 63244 (midnight blue).

❋ CALICO BIRD. French, c. 1780—90, block print with picotage. 100% cotton, glazed. 54″ wide, 14″ repeat. No. 70970 (document red).

❋ CHINESE BELLS. Probably French, c. 1770—80, block print. 100% cotton. 54″ wide, 28″ repeat. No. 70815 (document red).

❋ DIAMOND FLORAL. French (Provence), c. 1740—90, block print. 100% cotton. 54″ wide, 8″ repeat. No. 64714 (document rouge).

❋ HORSE AND FOX. English, c. 1770, copperplate print. 100% cotton. 36″ wide, 37″ repeat. No. 151572 (toile red).

❋ INDIAN FLOWERS. Indian, c. 1750—60, block print. 100% cotton. 54″ wide, 12¼″ repeat. No. 67754 (tile).

❋ JARDIN CHINOIS. English or French, c. 1760—80, block print. 54″ wide, 13″ repeat. No. 67740 (document blue and red).

❋ JONES TOILE. English, c. 1761, copperplate print. Victoria and Albert Museum, *English Printed Textiles,* pl. 4; Montgomery, *Printed Textiles,* fig. 214. 100% cotton. 40″ wide, 77″ repeat. The earliest dated copperplate-printed textile; inscribed "R. JONES, OLD FORD, 1761." Document a 19th-century reproduction of this design, used for bed hangings at Colonial Williamsburg. No. 152552 (toile red); No. 50092 (brick red).

❋ LOZENGE FLORAL. French, c. 1780, block print. 100% cotton. 54″ wide, 13½″ repeat. No. 73770 (document blue and red).

❋ PINEAPPLE AND POPPY. English, c. 1780—90, block print. 100% cotton. 64″ wide, 25¼″ repeat. No. 71530 (document red).

40

LOZENGE FLORAL,
c. 1780. Schumacher.
Document blue and red.

PINEAPPLE AND POPPY,
c. 1780–90. Schumacher.
Document red.

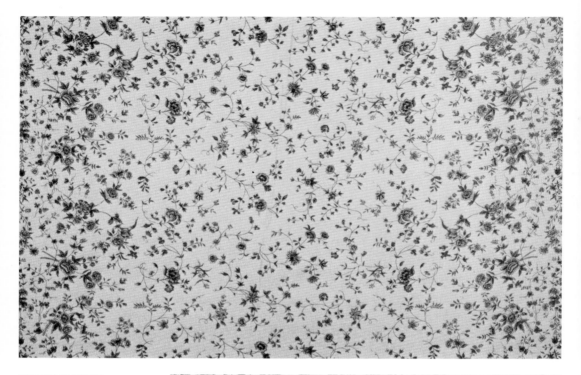

PONDI CHERRY,
c. 1750–1800.
Schumacher. Red.

SPRING FLOWERS,
c. 1775–80. Schumacher.
Document blue.

❋ PINTADO STRIPE. French, c. 1775, block print. 100% cotton. 36″ wide, 11½″ repeat. No. 50732 (document red and blue).

❋ PLANTATION CALICO. French, c. 1785, block print. 100% cotton. 50′ ′wide, 13¼″ repeat. No. 178062 (toile red).

❋ PLEASURES OF THE FARM. French (Jouy), c. 1783, copperplate print. Clouzot, pl. 18; Edwards and Ramsey, *Etoffes Imprimées Français,* no. 98. 100% cotton. 40″ wide, 40″ repeat. Design by Jean Baptiste Huet. No. 50428 (royal purple).

❋ PONDI CHERRY. Indian, c. 1750–1800, block print. 100% cotton. 54″ wide, 17¼″ repeat. No. 65100 (red).

❋ RALEIGH TAVERN RESIST. French, c. 1760–1800, resist print. 70% linen, 30% cotton. 48″ wide, 42″ repeat. No. 178164 (blue).

❋ SPRING FLOWERS. English, c. 1775–80, copperplate print. 100% cotton. 54″ wide, 21¾″ repeat. No. 73810 (document blue).

❋ STRING OF PEARLS. English or French, c. 1780, block print. 100% cotton. 54″ wide, 35″ repeat. No. 71170 (document burgundy).

❋ TRACERY FLORAL. French, c. 1770–1800, block print. 100% cotton. 54″ wide, 12⅝″ repeat. No. 73780 (document red).

❋ WILLIAMSBURG APPLES. French, c. 1750–80, block print. 100% linen. 48″ wide, 7″ repeat. Document originally used for a quilt lining. No. 60142 (brick). Adaptation 100% cotton, 54″ wide; No. 30502 (red).

❋ WILLIAMSBURG BLUEBELL STRIPE. French or English, c. 1770, block print. 100% cotton. 54″ wide, 1¾″ repeat. No. 66616 (rust and blue).

TRACERY FLORAL, c. 1770-1800. Schumacher. Document red.

❀ WILLIAMSBURG FLORAL STRIPE. French, c. 1785–1800, copperplate print. 100% cotton. 32″ wide, 12½″ repeat. No. 56333 (red on white).

❀ WILLIAMSBURG FLORAL TRAILS. English, c. 1770, copperplate print. 100% cotton. 54″ wide, 32″ repeat. Original attributed to the Ware Factory, Crayford, Kent. No. 60534 (blue).

❀ WILLIAMSBURG IRIS. English, c. 1780–85, copperplate print. Montgomery, *Printed Textiles*, fig. 238 and pl. 23. 100% cotton. 54″ wide, 36½″ repeat. Original printed at Bromley Hall, Middlesex. No. 67760 (document red).

❀ WILLIAMSBURG POMEGRANATE RESIST. Probably French, c. 1740–90, resist print. 70% linen, 30% cotton. 50″ wide, 20½″ repeat. No. 162694 (blue).

❀ WOOD FLORAL. English, c. 1785–1800, block print with picotage. 100% cotton. 54″ wide, 16″ repeat. No. 65062 (document blue and red).

WOVEN DESIGNS

BRUNSCHWIG AND FILS

❀ BOSCOBEL STRIPED LAMPAS. French, late 18th century. Reproduced for Boscobel Restoration, Garrison-on-Hudson, N.Y. Document in Brunschwig Archives. Special order only.

❀ CASTETS SILK DAMASK. French, c. 1700–40. 70% silk, 30% cotton. 50″ wide, 28″ repeat. Document privately owned in France. No. 100581.00 (red); No. 100584.00 (green); No. 100583.00 (yellow).

❀ MARIGNAN DAMASK. French, c. 1660–1800. 49% bemberg, 51% cotton. 50″ wide, 25½″ repeat. Document privately owned in France. No. 181753.00 (yellow).

❀ MOULINS DAMASK. French, mid-18th century. 72% cotton, 28% silk. 48″ wide, 18″ repeat. Document privately owned in France. No. 31630.00 (vieux rouge, No. 7208).

❀ PENELOPE BROCADE. French, c. 1760–90, brocaded wool flowers on fustian. 38% wool, 27% cotton, 35% linen. 51″ wide, 20½″ repeat. Document privately owned in France. No. 32630.00 (cream).

❀ TOILE PROVENCALE. French, c. 1780–1800, brocaded wool flowers on fustian. 15% wool, 42% cotton, 43% linen. 51″ wide, 15¾″ repeat. Handwoven. Document privately owned in France. No. 32405.00 (pink stripes); No. 32402.00 (blue stripes).

DECORATORS WALK

❀ CARLTON DAMAS. English or French, c. 1750–1800. 100% rayon. 56″ wide, 21″ repeat. From a privately owned silk document. No. P34884 (taupe); additional colors available.

❀ CASA SILK DAMASK. English or French, c. 1740–1800. 60% silk, 40% rayon. 50″ wide, 23″ repeat. From a silk document owned by J. H. Thorp and Company. No. T33700 (red).

❀ GAINSBOROUGH DAMASK. English, c. 1740–90. 100% cotton. 53″ wide, 27⅜″ repeat. From a privately owned silk document. No. P34812 (cranberry); 8 additional colors.

WOOD FLORAL,
c. 1785–1800.
Schumacher. Document
blue and red.

GEORGIAN DAMASK,
c. 1750–90. Scalamandré.
Georgian red.

❀ GEORGIAN DAMASK. English, c. 1750–1800. 60% silk, 40% rayon. 50″ wide, 25″ repeat. From a silk document owned by J. H. Thorp and Company. No. T34334 (peacock blue); additional colors available.

❀ TULLERIE BROCADE. French, c. 1760–90. 54% rayon, 46% cotton. 49″ wide, 25¼″ repeat. From a privately owned silk document. No. T31695 (multi on ivory).

❀ WILLIAMSBURG DAMASK. English, c. 1740–1800. 100% silk. 50″ wide, 27″ repeat. Document privately owned. No. L56486 (red).

LEE JOFA

Handwoven damasks are available by special order in four qualities: 100% heavy silk; 100% silk; 56.5% cotton, 43.5% silk; and 100% cotton. Minimum order 22 yards. Any color can be matched. Normal delivery time is 12 to 16 weeks; fabric is woven in England. The following designs are especially good for 18th-century work:

❀ BINGHAM. English, mid-18th century. 50″ wide, 55″ repeat. Document privately owned in England. No. L53-4.

❀ HAMPTON COURT PALACE. English, c. 1675–1750. 50″ wide, 44½″ repeat. Document privately owned in England. No. L12-15A.

❀ LIVERPOOL DAMASK. English, c. 1730–70. 50″ wide, 26″ repeat. Document privately owned in England. No. L6-1.

❀ PAVAI DAMASK. English, c. 1740–70. 50″ wide, 44¾″ repeat. Document privately owned in England. No. L3-1.

OLD WORLD WEAVERS

❋ DECATUR DAMASK. Italian, 18th century. 80% silk, 20% rayon. 50″wide, 27½″repeat. No. A-162-1808-1483 (color to order).

❋ DUQUESNE. French, 18th century. 40% silk, 60% rayon. 50″wide, 28″repeat. No. S-5203 (gold).

SCALAMANDRÉ

❋ CHINOISERIE DAMASK. English, c. 1730–50. 100% silk. 51″wide, 10″repeat. Document owned by Scalamandré. No. 90014-11 (old gold).

❋ CHINOISERIE DAMASK. English, c. 1740–60. 33% silk, 67% cotton. 51″ wide, 22½″ repeat. Document owned by Scalamandré. No. 99010-1 (beige and yellow).

❋ CHINOISERIE DAMASK. French, c. 1730. 100% silk. 50″wide, 18″ repeat. Document at the Louvre. No. 2733-9 (ivory and pale blue).

❋ CHINOISERIE LAMPAS. French or Italian, c. 1760. 100% silk. 50″ wide, 53″ repeat. Document owned by Scalamandré. No. 1495-4 (green). Document color special order only.

❋ DAMAS DE PARIS. French, 18th century. 100% silk. 51″wide, 21″ repeat. Document owned by Scalamandré. No. 97156-1 (wine); other colors available under series 97416.

❋ 18TH CENTURY CHARLESTON DAMASK. English, mid-18th century. 100% silk. 51″wide, 46½″repeat. Document owned by Edmondston-Alston House, Charleston. No. 2099-2 (kelly green).

❋ XVIII CENTURY DAMASK. English, c. 1750–1830. 100% silk. 50″ wide, 14½″repeat. Document privately owned. No. 2735-1 (crimson).

❋ FERRONERIE VELVET. Italian, c. 1760. 40% silk, 60% cotton. 23″ wide, 23″repeat. Document at Academy of Fine Arts, Philadelphia. No. 3154-4 (blue, gothic). Handwoven in Italy. Special order only; minimum order 10 yards.

❋ FLEUR RENAISSANCE. French or Italian, c. 1750–70. 100% silk. 51″ wide, 4⅛″ repeat. Document owned by Scalamandré. No. 370-16 (ivory and eggshell).

❋ FRENCH DAMASK. French, c. 1730–70. 100% silk. 50″wide, 36″ repeat. Document at Musée des Tissus, Paris. No. 360-2 (red).

❋ GEORGIAN ANTIQUE DAMASK. Italian, c. 1650–1775. 40% silk, 60% linen. 50″ wide, 24¼″ repeat. Document privately owned. No. 5138-9 (beige and white).

❋ GEORGIAN DAMASK. English, c. 1750–90. 100% silk. 50″wide, 24½″repeat. Document privately owned. No. 1225-23 (Georgian red); other 18th-century colors available.

❋ LOUIS XVI DAMASK. French, c. 1770–1800. 89% silk, 11% cotton. 51½″wide, 32″repeat. Document owned by Scalamandré. No. 97362-1 (gray on blue).

❋ LOUIS XVI LAMPAS. French, c. 1770–1800. 100% silk. 50″wide, 27″repeat. Document privately owned. No. 535-1 (beige, gold and red). Handwoven in Italy. Special order only.

NATCHEZ XVIII
CENTURY LAMPAS,
c. 1740–90. Scalamandré.
Blue and off-white.

✿ LOVE BIRD DAMASK. Italian, c. 1650–1750. 100% silk. 50" wide, 18½" repeat. Document owned by Scalamandré. No. 1098-3 (blue).

✿ MARY TODD LINCOLN DAMASK. French, c. 1750–1800. 100% silk. 50" wide, 30¼" repeat. Document owned by Scalamandré. No. 4986-3 (wine). Also woven with a 23½" repeat; No. 4986-4 (ivory and gold).

✿ METROPOLITAN MUSEUM OF ART DAMASK. French or English, c. 1750–1850. 30% silk, 70% cotton. 50" wide, 24" repeat. Document owned by Scalamandré. No. 1348-14 (burgundy).

✿ MET ORIENTAL DAMASK. French, c. 1730–50. 32% silk, 68% cotton. 50¾" wide, 28¾" repeat. Document at Metropolitan Museum of Art. No. 97383-1 (old gold).

✿ NATCHEZ XVIII CENTURY LAMPAS. French, c. 1740–90. 100% silk. 50" wide, 29" repeat. Document owned by Scalamandré. No. 1493-6 (blue and off-white).

✿ POTTSGROVE DAMASK. French, 18th century. 100% silk. 50" wide, 17" repeat. Document owned by Scalamandré. No. 166-1 (gold).

✿ RESTORATION DAMASK. French or English, mid-18th century. 26% silk, 74% cotton. 50" wide, 53" repeat. Document owned by Scalamandré. No. 638-30 (gold).

MARY TODD LINCOLN
DAMASK, c.1750–1800.
Scalamandré. Wine.

POTTSGROVE DAMASK,
18th century. Scalamandré.
Gold.

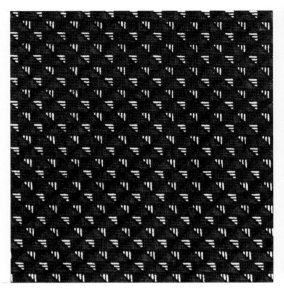

top left
WICKER VELVERETTE,
c. 1750–70. Schumacher.
Document green and brown.

top right
RUTHMERE DAMASK,
18th century. Scalamandré.
Old gold.

right
VENETIAN DAMASK,
1650–present.
Scalamandré. Beige on
peach.

❋ RUTHMERE DAMASK. English, 18th century. 100% silk. 51"wide, 45"repeat. Document privately owned. No. 97292-1 (old gold). Special order only.

❋ SAN GALLEN DAMASK. French, c. 1700–50. 100% silk. 51½" wide, 20"repeat. Document owned by Scalamandré. No. 97415-1 (golden cream and champagne).

❋ XVII CENTURY ANTIQUE DAMASK. English, c. 1750. 38% silk, 62% linen. 50"wide, 34"repeat. Document at Gunston Hall, Fairfax County, Va. No. 90022-2 (green and ivory).

❋ STRATFORD DAMASK. French or English, c. 1740–70. 100% silk. 50"wide, 21½"repeat. Document privately owned. No. 526-12 (gold strié).

❋ VENETIAN DAMASK. Italy, c. 1650–present. 77% silk, 23% rayon. 51"wide, 15"repeat. Document at Victoria and Albert Museum. No. 97386-1 (beige on peach).

SCHUMACHER
COLONIAL WILLIAMSBURG REPRODUCTIONS

All documents are in the textile collection of Colonial Williamsburg, Williamsburg, Va. For this group of fabrics the term "document" refers to a reproduction made of the same fiber as the original document; the term "adaptation" is used to refer to a reproduction that carefully reproduces the design, scale and color of the original textile but is made of different fibers. Both are acceptable for restoration work.

❋ BRUTON ADAPTATION DAMASK. c. 1740–75. 67% mercerized cotton, 33% silk. 52"wide, 21¼"repeat. No. 33101 (gold).

❋ GREEN SPRING DAMASK DOCUMENT. Italian, mid-17th century. 100% silk. 54"wide, 8"repeat. No. 34520 (green).

❋ GREEN SPRING ADAPTATION DAMASK. Italian, mid-17th century. 74% spun rayon, 26% silk. 54"wide, 8"repeat. No. 34531 (gold).

❋ LIVERPOOL BIRDS. English, c. 1760–90. 100% cotton. 54"wide, 7" repeat. No. 131123 (bois).

❋ LUDWELL ADAPTATION DAMASK. French or Italian, early to mid-18th century. 100% cotton. 53" wide, 18" repeat. No. 31084 (opaline blue).

❋ WICKER VELVERETTE. English, c. 1750–70. 100% cotton. 54" wide, all-over repeat. No. 70217 (document green and brown).

❋ WILLIAMSBURG GARDEN DAMASK. French, c. 1750. 100% cotton. 54"wide, 21"vertical repeat. 13½"horizontal repeat. No. 51M620 (ivory).

100% cotton. 50" wide, 18¾" repeat. Document privately owned in France. No. 173370.00 (multi on beige).

❁ MARLBORO COTTON PRINT. English, c. 1805–07, block print. 100% cotton. 54" wide, 11¼" repeat. Document owned by Winterthur Museum. No. 77183.04 (aubergine and gold).

❁ MIREILLE. French (Alsace), late 18th century, block print. 100% cotton. 50" wide, 8½" repeat. Document privately owned in France. No. 173825.00 (coral and olive on brown).

❁ NEW ZINNIA TOILE. French or English, late 18th century, copperplate print. 100% cotton. 55" wide, 39½" repeat. Document privately owned. No. 67282.01 (blue on white).

❁ OGDEN HOUSE GLAZED CHINTZ. English, c. 1814, block print. 100% cotton, glazed. 33" wide, 15½" repeat. Original design slightly diminished. Document in Brunschwig Archives. No. 77778.04 (multi on yellow). Special order only.

❁ OSTERLEY. English, c. 1805–10, block print. 100% cotton, glazed. 45½" wide plus 8½" border on one side, 14¼" repeat. Document in Brunschwig Archives. Matching pairs of original window curtains made from this fabric are in collections of Victoria and Albert Museum and Old Sturbridge Village, Sturbridge, Mass. No. 77063.04 (yellow).

❁ PROVENCAL COTTON PRINT. French (Jouy), c. 1795, block print. *Chefs d'Oeuvre du Musée de l'Impression sur Etoffes, Mulhouse*, vol. 3, fig. 116; d'Allemagne, pl. 18. 100% cotton. 54" wide, 11" repeat. Document at Musée de l'Impression sur Etoffes, Mulhouse, France. No. 61291.01 (red).

❁ SALEM TAVERN STRIPE. Possibly American, late 18th century, block print. 100% cotton. 48" wide, 1" repeat. Original fabric part of woman's pocket found in North Carolina; one of several fabrics used as patchwork making up the front of pocket. Document owned by Museum of Early Southern Decorative Arts. No. 73358.04 (brown and beige on white).

❁ SCENES PAYSANNES. French, early 19th century, block print. 100% cotton. 54½" wide, 25½" repeat. Document privately owned in France. No. 174201.00 (red and blue).

❁ SHELL TOILE. English, late 18th century, copperplate print. Montgomery, *Printed Textiles*, fig. 242. 100% cotton. 54" wide, 32½" repeat. Reproduced for Liberty Hall Restoration, Kenansville, N.C. Document in Brunschwig Archives. No. 72178.04 (brown on white).

❁ STONEHOUSE STRIPE. French, late 18th century, block print. 100% cotton. 48½" wide, 12⅝" repeat. Reproduced for Hezekiah Alexander House, Charlotte, N.C. Document in Brunschwig Archives. No. 76907.04 (plum, tan and blue).

❁ SUN, MOON AND STARS GLAZED CHINTZ. English, c. 1790–1820, block print. 100% cotton. 49" wide, 9" repeat. Scale slightly altered. Document in Winterthur Museum. No. 78407.04 (red on beige).

OSTERLEY, c. 1805–10.
Brunschwig and Fils.
Yellow.

NEW ZINNIA TOILE, late
18th century. Brunschwig
and Fils. Blue on white.

MARLBORO COTTON
PRINT, c. 1805—07.
Brunschwig and Fils.
Aubergine and gold.

SHELL TOILE, late 18th
century. Brunschwig and
Fils. Brown on white.

top left
COMPAGNE DES INDES,
late 18th century. Clarence
House. Rouge.

top right
BUCKINGHAM TOILE
PRINT, c. 1790–95. Lee
Jofa. Blue.

right
APHRODITE TOILE,
c. 1790. Scalamandré. Blue
on white.

❋ VILLEROY. French, late 18th century, block print. 56% cotton, 44% linen. 48″wide, 12½″repeat. Document in Brunschwig Archives. No. 73930.04 (red and blue on cream).

❋ VIVIENNE. French, late 18th century, block print. 100% cotton. 50″ wide, 8¼″repeat. Document privately owned in France. No. 173620.00 (multi on cream).

CLARENCE HOUSE

❋ COMPAGNE DES INDES. French, late 18th century, block print. 100% cotton. 46″ wide plus 4½″ border on each side, 26″ repeat. Document privately owned. No. 32043-1 (rouge). Minimum order two yards.

❋ INDUS. French, late 18th century, block print. 100% cotton, glazed. 55″wide, 21″repeat. Document privately owned. No. 32019-1 (multi). Minimum order two yards.

❋ JONQUERIE. French, late 18th century, block print. 100% cotton, glazed. 55″wide, 16½″repeat. Document privately owned. No. 31918-1 (bleu and rose). Minimum order two yards.

❋ PERSAN. French, late 18th century, block print. 100% cotton, glazed. 51″wide, 14¾″repeat. Document privately owned. No. 31688-5 (ecru). Minimum order two yards.

DECORATORS WALK

❋ LE TRIOMPHE DE L'HYMENEE. French (Nantes), 1795, copperplate print. D'Allemagne, pl. 107. 100% cotton. 36″ wide, 40″ repeat. Document a textile produced by Petitpierre and Company; now in textile collection of Metropolitan Museum of Art. No. 54692 (rose and brown).

LEE JOFA

❋ BUCKINGHAM TOILE PRINT. English, c. 1790–95, copperplate print. 100% cotton. 34″ wide, 34½″ half-drop repeat. Document owned by Lee Jofa. No. 8761-1 (blue); No. 8763-1 (red).

SCALAMANDRÉ

❋ ANDREW JACKSON CHINTZ. English, late 18th century, block print. 100% cotton. 50″ wide, 36″ repeat. Document owned by The Hermitage, Nashville. No. 6046-1 (multi on dark brown).

❋ APHRODITE TOILE. English, c. 1790, copperplate print. 100% linen. 48″ wide, 32½″ repeat. Document privately owned; said to have been used by Thomas Jefferson at Monticello, Charlottesville, Va. No. 6281-14 (blue on white). Special order only.

❋ BLIND MAN'S BUFF. English, late 18th century, copperplate print. Montgomery, *Printed Textiles*, fig. 288 (one motif). 100% linen. 50″ wide, 32″ repeat. Document privately owned. No. 6065-1 (brown on tan).

CLIVEDEN, CHEW
HOUSE PANEL, late 18th
century. Scalamandré.
Multi reds, blues, greens
and browns on ecru.

DOCUMENTARY PRINT,
c. 1790–1800.
Scalamandré. Pink, red
and brown on beige.

● CHARLESTON TOILE IMPRIMÉ. French or English, c. 1740–80, block print. 100% cotton, glazed. 54″ wide, 12½″ repeat. Document owned by Historic Charleston Foundation, Charleston, S.C. No. 7779-1 (chocolate, aqua and pink on ivory).

● CLIVEDEN, CHEW HOUSE PANEL. English, late 18th century, block print. 100% cotton. 36″ wide, 99″ pattern repeat printed with 14″ plain fabric at top and bottom; cut in 3½-yard panels only. Document a bed covering (perhaps originally window curtains) at Cliveden, Germantown, Pa. No. 6811-1 (multi reds, blues, greens and browns on ecru).

● COLONIAL TULIP. French (Mellier, Beautiran, near Bordeaux), 1810, block print (lapis style). D'Allemagne, fig. 23. 100% cotton. 50″ wide, 9¼″ repeat. Document owned by Scalamandré. No. 8341-8 (blues and red on plum).

● CURWEN BED HANGING. English, c. 1810, block print. Cummings, *Bed Hangings*, fig. 31. 100% cotton, glazed. 48″ wide, 30″ repeat. Document a complete set of original bed hangings in Essex Institute, Salem, Mass. No. 6827-1 (multi on cream).

● DIRECTOIRE TOILE. French (Jouy), c. 1805, copperplate print. Clouzot, pl. 20 ("Classic Medallions"). 100% cotton. 50″ wide, 14″ repeat. Document privately owned. No. 6447-1 (reds on white).

● DOCUMENTARY PRINT. English, c. 1790–1800, block print. 100% linen. 42″ wide, 34″ repeat. Document privately owned. No. 6295-10 (pink, red and brown on beige); white ground available by special order only.

FLORAL DESIGN,
c. 1790–1800.
Scalamandré. Red, green,
gold and brown on ecru.

❊ ELIZA LUCAS FLORAL. English, c. 1750–60, block print. 100% cotton. 54″ wide, 25¼″ repeat. Document owned by Historic Charleston Foundation, Charleston, S.C. No. 7780-1 (burgundies, browns, light blue and green on pongee).

❊ FERN AND THISTLE. English, late 18th century, copperplate print. 100% cotton. 48″ wide, 37″ repeat. Document privately owned. No. 6490-2 (blues on natural).

❊ FLORAL DESIGN. English, c. 1790–1800, block print. 100% cotton. 48″ wide, 27″ repeat. Adapted from textile document in Metropolitan Museum of Art. No. 6533-7 (red, green, gold and brown on ecru).

❊ METROPOLITAN POMEGRANATE. English, late 18th century, block print. 100% cotton, glazed. 48″ wide, 32½″ repeat. Adapted from textile document in Metropolitan Museum of Art. No. 6408-1 (reds, aquas and browns on ecru).

❊ ORIENTAL DIVERSIONS. French, late 18th century, block print. 100% cotton. 48″ wide, 15⅝″ repeat. Document owned by Scalamandré. No. 6405-1 (rose, blue and green on chocolate).

❊ OWENS THOMAS COVERLET. English, c. 1795–1810, copperplate print. 100% cotton. 33¾″ wide, 37″ repeat. Document a bed covering at Owens Thomas House, Savannah, Ga. No. 6489-1 (brown on ecru).

❊ QUAIL UNGLAZED CHINTZ. English, c. 1815–35, block print. 100% cotton. 47″ wide, 15½″ repeat. Document owned by Scalamandré. No. 6256-1 (multi on tan).

❊ REVOLUTIONARY TOILE. English, c. 1785–1800, copperplate

METROPOLITAN
POMEGRANATE, late 18th
century. Scalamandré.
Reds, aquas and browns
on ecru.

print. Montgomery, *Printed Textiles*, fig. 301 ("America Presenting at the Altar of Liberty Medallions of Her Illustrious Sons"). 100% cotton. 50″ wide, 30″ repeat. Document owned by Scalamandré. No. 6247-4 (reds on off-white).

❀ SUMMER FLORA. English, late 18th century, block print. 100% cotton. 48″ wide, 11″ repeat. Adapted from textile in Metropolitan Museum of Art. No. 6401-1 (red and blue on ecru).

❀ WOODBURY PRINT. English, early 19th century, resist print. 100% cotton. 40″ wide, 26″ repeat. Document in American Wing, Metropolitan Museum of Art. No. 6673-1 (light blue and dark blue on cream).

Schumacher
Colonial Williamsburg Reproductions
Unless otherwise cited, all documents are in the textile collection of Colonial Williamsburg, Williamsburg, Va.

❀ COTTON 54. Probably Dutch, c. 1800. 100% cotton. 54″ wide, all-over repeat. Document from a Dutch merchant's swatchbook. No. 75M900 (document charcoal).

❀ DANDELION. Probably Dutch, c. 1800. 100% cotton. 54″ wide, 1¼″ vertical repeat, 2¼″ horizontal repeat. Document from a Dutch merchant's swatchbook. No. 75M880 (document indigo and gold).

❀ FIELD. Probably Dutch, c. 1800. 100% cotton. 54″ wide, all-over stripes. Document from a Dutch merchant's swatchbook. No. 75M910 (document indigo and gold).

❀ FLOWER LEAF STRIPE. French, c. 1790–1830. 100% cotton. 54″ wide, 10⅛″ repeat. Document used as a quilt lining. No. 73800 (document red).

❀ GARDEN ROW. Probably Dutch, c. 1800. 100% cotton. 54″ wide, 2¾″ repeat. Document from a Dutch merchant's swatchbook. No. 75M890 (document charcoal).

❀ HEDGEROW. Probably Dutch, c. 1800. 100% cotton. 54″ wide, 4″ repeat. Document from a Dutch merchant's swatchbook. No. 75M840 (document indigo).

❀ MORNING GLORY. English, c. 1800, copperplate print. 100% cotton. 54″ wide, 36¼″ repeat. No. 70980 (document red).

❀ PARSLEY. Probably Dutch, c. 1800. 100% cotton. 54″ wide, 6″ repeat. Document from a Dutch merchant's swatchbook. No. 74250 (document blue).

❀ PILLEMENT. French, c. 1790–1815, block print. 100% cotton. 48″ wide, 16″ repeat. No. 70820 (document rose).

❀ SEEDPODS. Probably Dutch, c. 1800. 100% cotton. 54″ wide, 1¼″ vertical repeat, 1½″ horizontal repeat. Document from a Dutch merchant's swatchbook. No. 75M850 (document midnight blue).

❀ STARS. Probably Dutch, c. 1800. 100% cotton. 54″ wide, all-over repeat. Document from a Dutch merchant's swatchbook. No. 75M860 (document indigo and gold).

❀ WILLIAMSBURG FLOWERING TREE. English, c. 1800, block print. 100% cotton. 54″ wide, 34″ repeat. No. 60362 (ruby).

❀ WILLIAMSBURG GRAPES. English, c. 1790, block print. 100% cotton. 54″ wide, 17″ repeat. Document in Schumacher Collection. No. 64926 (document rust).

❀ WILLIAMSBURG POTPOURRI. English, c. 1815, block print. 100% cotton. 36″ wide, 22¼″ repeat. Adapted from document at Victoria and Albert Museum. No. 153033 (buff).

❀ WILLIAMSBURG SPRIG. Probably Dutch, c. 1800. 100% cotton. 54″ wide, all-over repeat. Document from a Dutch merchant's swatchbook. No. 75M920 (document indigo).

❀ WILLIAMSBURG VINEYARD. Probably Dutch, c. 1800. 100% cotton. 54″ wide, 7¼″ repeat. Document from a Dutch merchant's swatchbook. No. 75M870 (document midnight blue).

❀ WILLIAMSBURG WYTHE HOUSE BORDER RESIST. English or American, c. 1790–1800, resist dyed. 50″ wide, 28″ repeat. No. 162544 (blue).

WAVERLY FABRICS
OLD STURBRIDGE VILLAGE REPRODUCTIONS

❀ WILDWOOD. English or American, c. 1790–1800, block print. 100% cotton. 54″ wide, 4½″ repeat. Document a quilt lining in textile collection at Old Sturbridge Village, Sturbridge, Mass. No. 687721 (colonial red and blue).

FLOWER LEAF STRIPE,
c. 1790–1830. Schumacher.
Document red.

PARSLEY, c. 1800.
Schumacher. Document
blue.

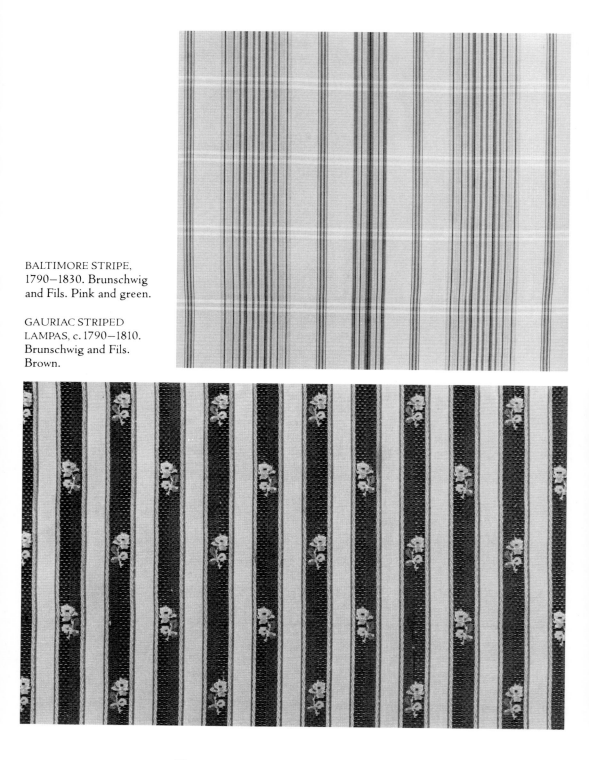

BALTIMORE STRIPE, 1790–1830. Brunschwig and Fils. Pink and green.

GAURIAC STRIPED LAMPAS, c. 1790–1810. Brunschwig and Fils. Brown.

BRUNSCHWIG AND FILS

❀ AGEN BROCADE. French, c. 1800–15. 100% rayon. 50″ wide, 5¼″ repeat. Silk document privately owned in France. No. 121230.00 (gold on cream ground); No. 121231.00 (gold on red ground).

❀ BALTIMORE STRIPE. European, 1790–1830. 100% rayon. 50″ wide. Silk document owned by Winterthur Museum. No. 64895.01 (pink and green).

❀ GAURIAC STRIPED LAMPAS. French, c. 1790–1810. 100% silk. 21″ wide, 3″ repeat. Document privately owned in France. No. 33768.00 (brown).

❀ LAUREAL DAMASK. French, c. 1790–1810. 60% spun rayon, 40% nylon. 52″ wide, 27″ repeat. Silk document at Museum of Early Southern Decorative Arts. No. 10009.02 (white on beige).

❀ LESPARRE. French, early 19th century, woven stripe. 100% rayon. 48″ wide. Reproduced for Liberty Hall, Kenansville, N.C. Silk document privately owned. No. 30942.00 (blue and cream).

❀ ST. CYR. French, c. 1790–1810, brocaded satin. 70% spun rayon, 30% bemberg. 50″ wide, 10¼″ repeat. Silk document at Musée des Arts Décoratifs, Paris. No. 142231.00 (red ground with black and white tails).

DECORATORS WALK

❀ NAPOLEON BEE DAMASK. French, c. 1800–15. 100% silk. 50″ wide, 3½″ repeat. Document privately owned. No. L57835 (yellow and white).

LEE JOFA

❀ LAMPAS BONAPARTE. French, c. 1800–10. 100% rayon. 50″ wide. Based on silk document owned by Lee Jofa. No. J67040 (cream); No. J67041 (green).

SCALAMANDRÉ

❀ ADAM DAMASK. English, late 18th century. 100% silk. 50″ wide, 18″ repeat. Document at Monticello, Charlottesville, Va. No. 1384-12 (burgundy).

❀ "THE BEE" NAPOLEON LAMPAS. French or Italian, c. 1790–1815. 25% silk, 75% rayon. 50″ wide, 3½″ repeat. Silk document privately owned in Italy. No. 96103-2 (beige and gold on oriental blue).

❀ BROGART D'AVIGNON. Italian, c. 1790–1850. 100% silk. 50″ wide, 7″ repeat. Handwoven brocade. Document privately owned in Italy. No. 96134-1 (multi on rose and brown vertical stripes).

❀ DUMBARTON DAMASK. French or English, c. 1790–1820. 30% silk, 70% spun rayon. 51″ wide, 5″ repeat. Document owned by Scalamandré. No. 97382-1 (gold).

❀ EMPIRE LAMPAS. French, c. 1805–30. 100% silk. 51″ wide, 36″ repeat. No. 451-1 (yellow and persian rose). Special order only.

❋ EMPIRE LAMPAS. French, c. 1805. 100% silk. 50" wide, 16" repeat. Document privately owned in France. Yardage No. 97052-1. Chair seat, 31" wide, 25" long, No. 97053-1. Chair backs, 26" wide, 25" long, No. 97054-1. Sofa panel, 2½ yards wide, 25" long, No. 97055-1. All royal gold on regal red.

❋ FEDERAL LAMPAS. French, early 19th century. 75% silk, 25% cotton. 50" wide, 7¼" repeat. Document privately owned. No. 1951-1 (federal gold on sage). Special order only.

❋ GARDNER MUSEUM. French, early 19th century, lampas. 75% silk, 25% cotton. Reproduced for Isabella Stuart Gardner Museum, Boston. Chair back, 50" wide, 2½ yards long with two motifs across width and 9" plain satin between, 12" plain satin below and 62" plain satin above, No. 97232-1. Chair seat, 50" wide, 2½ yards long, with two motifs across width and 9" plain satin between, 12" plain satin below and 62" plain satin above. Both cut by repeat only. Coordinating fabric "Emperor Lampas," 50½" wide, 4¼" repeat. No. 97218-1. All silver on royal. Other colors by special order.

❋ GERMANTOWN STRIPE. French or English, c. 1790–1850, taffeta. 100% silk. 52" wide. Document at Cliveden, Germantown, Pa. No. 99460-1 (cranberry and apple green).

❋ LOUIS XIV LAMPAS. French, late 18th century. 100% silk. 50" wide, 69" repeat. Document at Monticello, Charlottesville, Va. No. 1496 (blue and silver).

❋ METROPOLITAN ROSETTE EMPIRE LAMPAS. French, late 18th century. 100% silk. 50" wide, 16" repeat. Document owned by Scalamandré. No. 97228-1 (golds on royal red).

❋ MUSEUM DAMASK. French, late 18th century. 26% silk, 74% cotton. 51" wide, 12½" repeat. Document owned by Scalamandré. No. 1622-3 (blue and ivory).

❋ NAPOLEON DAMASK. French, late 18th or early 19th century. 33% silk, 67% cotton. 50" wide, 9" repeat. Document privately owned. No. 96290-1 (gold and green strié on putty).

❋ OAK HILL DAMASK. Probably French, c. 1810–20. 100% silk. 51" wide, 12" repeat. Document at Essex Institute, Salem, Mass. No. 96398-1 (salmon).

❋ POMPEIAN MEMORIES DAMASK. English, c. 1790–1800. 70% cotton, 30% silk. 56" wide, 17" repeat. Document owned by Scalamandré. No. 97412-1 (golden honey).

❋ STRIPED TAFFETA. English or French, c. 1790–1830. 100% silk. 50" wide. Document privately owned. No. 90010-2 (multi orange, gold, green and yellow).

SCHUMACHER
COLONIAL WILLIAMSBURG REPRODUCTIONS

❋ FLEURETTE DOCUMENT. French or English, c. 1790–1810. 100% silk. 54" wide, 3½" repeat. Document at Colonial Williamsburg,

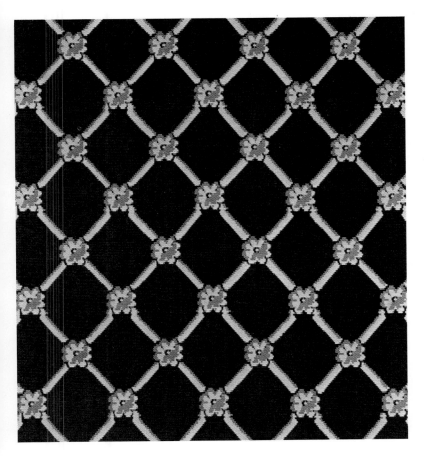

EMPEROR LAMPAS, early 19th century. Scalamandré. Silver on royal. See "Gardner Museum."

Williamsburg, Va. No. 36820 (document blue).

🏵 WILLIAMSBURG MULTI STRIPE. French or English, c. 1790–1800. 100% cotton. 52" wide, 6½" horizontal repeat. Document at Colonial Williamsburg, Williamsburg, Va. No. 132962 (red).

STROHEIM AND ROMANN

🏵 AVALON. French, c. 1790–1830, woven stripe. 60% spun rayon, 40% cotton. 54" wide. Adapted from a 100% silk bourette in the collection of Winterthur Museum. No. 39575–39579 series (document red and green).

WAVERLY FABRICS
OLD STURBRIDGE VILLAGE REPRODUCTIONS

🏵 THOMAS SHERATON DAMASK. Probably English, early 19th century. 100% cotton. 48" wide, 3¼" repeat. Adapted from scarlet wool damask window curtain at Old Sturbridge Village, Sturbridge, Mass. No. 642287 (scarlet).

69

1815 TO 1840:
TECHNOLOGICAL ADVANCES
AND COMPLEX DESIGNS

During the years 1815–40, the development of power looms, the perfection of cylinder printing and continuing improvements in dye technology greatly changed the textile industry in Europe and the United States. The broad-scale adoption of the Jacquard selective shedding device for pattern weaving allowed increasing complexity in woven silk and woolen designs. The use of engraved metal cylinders for printing meant that design repeats were shorter and motifs often finely drawn. Popular designs included floral stripes, shells and coral branches, birds and elaborately foliated pillar prints. The practice of outlining or emphasizing design motifs with clusters of small dots was even more common than in the previous period. For a time there was also a revival of monochromatic landscapes and commemorative designs in a style highly reminiscent of the earlier copperplate designs but now made much denser and with the shorter repeat defined by the circumference of the printing cylinder. Block printing continued to be used for large-scale floral chintzes. (For more details see Florence Montgomery, *Printed Textiles*, pages 287–343.)

London and Paris continued to be the primary sources of new ideas about interior decoration. Travelers paid particular attention to the opulent interiors they visited, and they consulted with merchants, designers and fabric suppliers about appropriate styles and newly available goods. Sometimes Americans commissioned their friends or relatives who were traveling or living abroad to send them new fabrics or even new curtains and furniture coverings in the latest style, not knowing what they might receive.

The number of published design books also increased during this period. Volumes such as Pierre de la Messangere's *Meubles et Objets de Gout* and George Smith's *A Collection of Designs for Household Furniture* provided written descriptions as well as detailed illustrations, often in vivid color, of the new styles of French drapery and Grecian, Egyptian or Gothic taste. Selections from the most notable of these books are illustrated in Samuel J. Dornsife's "Design Sources for Nineteenth-Century Window Hangings."

In addition to books devoted exclusively to furniture and furnishing

PARTERRE, c. 1835.
Brunschwig and Fils.
Multi.

71

designs, fashionable periodicals featured illustrations of interior furnishings. Notable among them was Rudolph Ackermann's monthly *Repository of Arts, Literature, Commerce, Manufactures, Fashion and Politics* (London, 1809–28), which contained colored illustrations of fashionable clothing and furnishings, the latter often being window drapery. For a brief period, Ackermann even included actual textile swatches as emblems of British manufacturers. Surviving today, unfaded between the pages of the magazine, they offer an excellent idea of the brilliant color and glossy finish deemed ideal in furnishing fabrics at this time.

During the 1820s there appeared the first of the domestic advice books, the forerunners of the avalanche of texts providing detailed information on American material culture and social behavior in the late 19th and the 20th centuries. Among the earliest of these handbooks was *Domestic Duties, or Instructions to Young Married Ladies,* by Mrs. William Parkes. An American edition of this book was published in 1829, with few changes from the London original. Mrs. Parkes offered specific guidelines on the appropriateness of specific fabrics for specific rooms: Light-colored chintz or silk drapery with muslin undercurtains was approved for parlors; in contrast, the more severe wool moreen curtains in crimson or scarlet were deemed appropriate for dining rooms. Moreen was also considered suitable for bedchambers, although light-colored chintz prints with contrasting linings were also regarded as handsome. Dimity was admired for bedchambers, sometimes in combination with Marseilles spreads.

Paintings and drawings of American interiors began to be more common than they had been in the 18th century. These often depicted the use of textiles in decorating the parlors, sitting rooms and, occasionally, the bedchambers of middle-class and wealthy Americans. Woodcut illustrations in magazines and juvenile books also appeared with increasing frequency, often documenting the appearance of rooms of average Americans and sometimes those of lower socioeconomic levels. An excellent overview is given in *A Documentary History of American Interiors,* by Edgar Mayhew and Minor Myers.

The period 1815–40 saw the beginnings of the historical revival styles that were to characterize interior decorating throughout the remainder of the 19th century. Grecian and Egyptian designs had been used since the start of the century, but by the mid-1820s published designs for Gothic, Louis XIV, Louis XV and Elizabethan window drapery were also available. Such designs often made use of sheer white cotton curtains against the window panes; above these, special decorative effects were created by layers of heavier fabric and shaped valances. Where French drapery continued to be used, the swags and cascades became increasingly complex, enhanced by the use of contrasting linings and elaborate trimmings.

In 1833 J. C. Loudon's *Encyclopaedia of Cottage, Farm and Villa Architecture and Furniture* offered specific illustrations of the currently popular styles adapted for people of varying economic levels. The simplest designs illustrated by Loudon are for straight hanging panels of heavy material, hung from large brass or wooden rings on visible rods with boldly turned finials. Straight or shaped valances could be hung over these to give Grecian or Gothic effects. These basic designs must have been especially popular in houses of middle-class Americans during the second quarter of the 19th century, for as late as 1849 they were still being illustrated as fashionable in *Godey's Lady's Book*.

Apparently chintz and dimity were relegated to the bedchamber during most of this period, although even there embossed moreen, silk or other solid-colored fabrics might be used for bed and window hangings. As late as 1851, in an edition of the *Treatise on Domestic Economy*, Catherine Beecher was still urging that all fabric furnishings in a bedchamber should correspond.

The use of bed hangings was a matter of individual choice that reflected patterns of fashion as well as philosophies of hygiene. Throughout the 1830s and 1840s controversy raged over the healthfulness of fully enclosing bed curtains. In 1839 Sarah Josepha Hale, editor of *Godey's*, wrote, "Bed hangings are unhealthy. They confine the air about us while we sleep." At the same time decorators and designers were publishing new designs for bed hangings, which were being used in many fashionable and common chambers. In some cases these were strictly a decorative display on the posts and tester frame, but some people continued the old-fashioned practice of closing bed curtains around them at night, especially during cold weather. Lightweight bobbinet or gauze was used in a similar way in southern climates as a protection against mosquitoes; often heavier curtains were hung over the mosquito curtain in fashionable drapery styles.

Research in probate inventories that record domestic furnishings in rural areas shows that throughout this period the houses of most middle-class people — both farmers and village artisans — still had no window curtains. If curtains were used at all, they were usually used in the parlor. In restoring and furnishing a simple rural house of this period, two approaches are correct: using no window curtains or using only single white cotton panels swagged to one side in a way reminiscent of the 18th-century style called half drapery.

Roller blinds were introduced at least as early as 1825. They were tacked to wooden dowels supported by simple brackets or fitted within fixed pulleys. The spring blind was not invented until the end of this period. The blinds could be made of plain white cotton or brown holland (unbleached linen), or they could be embellished with colorful painted transparent landscapes. (Excellent reproductions of the latter style can be ordered through the Museum Gift Shop, Old Sturbridge Village, Sturbridge, Mass. 01566.)

The increasing use of upholstered furniture during this period resulted in some specific fabrics being made as furniture covers, but in many houses the same wools and silks were used for drapery in parlors or sitting rooms. Plain or patterned horsehair fabric was also used extensively for this purpose. Special panels were woven for the seats and backs of chairs and Grecian sofas; these are found in silk, wool and horsehair. No reproductions of the special wool or horsehair panels are currently available, but there is an excellent choice of woven silk panels. Also available are embossing designs that can be applied to wool or plush for seating furniture.

Slipcovers continued to be used in warm weather as a protection for expensive upholstery fabrics and to present a crisp, cool appearance. Undoubtedly, they were also used because they provided a much more comfortable sitting surface than wool or horsehair. Figured chintzes and dimity continued to be popular for this purpose, and by the mid-1830s crisp stripes of white and red, blue or green were also used.

The growing fashion for center tables in parlors fostered the production of specific kinds of woven or printed woolen table covers, none of which is reproduced today. Fortunately, some people made their own center table covers of plain woolen fabric trimmed with plain or patterned woven tapes, an effect easily recreated from commercially available goods.

The options for reproducing an accurate interior for the period 1815–40 are greater than for reproducing one of the earlier periods. Thus, it is even more important to decide in advance the purpose of the restoration and the point of view to be indicated in the fabric furnishings. A wide variety of handsome and appropriate effects can be created from period designs and available materials. Because so many effects are appropriate, selecting a focus is critical.

PRINTS

BRUNSCHWIG AND FILS

✹ BERMUDA CORAL GLAZED CHINTZ. English, c. 1830, block and roller print. 100% cotton, glazed. 50" wide, 4" repeat. Document privately owned in England. No. 65980.01 (red and green on cream).

✹ BRAHMAPOUTRA SATEEN PRINT. French (Alsace), c. 1830, block and discharge print. 100% cotton. 51" wide, 7" repeat. Document privately owned in France. No. 174041.00 (red).

✹ CHINESE LEOPARD TOILE. French, c. 1825, roller print. 100% cotton. 36" wide, 15¼" repeat. Document privately owned. No. 70121.04 (shades of red and blue).

✹ CORAL BRANCH GLAZED CHINTZ. English, c. 1825–50, roller and block print. 100% cotton. 44" wide plus one 6¾" side border, 12¾" repeat. Document in Brunschwig Archives. No. 78221.04 (red and blue).

✹ CORAUX GLAZED CHINTZ. French (Alsace), c. 1835, block print. 100% cotton, glazed. 51" wide, 5¾" repeat. Document at Musée des Arts Décoratifs, Paris. No. 61582.01 (blue).

✹ CUSTOM HOUSE GLAZED CHINTZ. English, c. 1820–30, roller print. 100% cotton, glazed. 55" wide, 12½" repeat. Document owned by Society for the Preservation of Long Island Antiquities, Setauket, N.Y. No. 77058.04 (brown and apricot).

CORAUX GLAZED
CHINTZ, c. 1835.
Brunschwig and Fils. Blue.

NANCRAY, c.1830.
Brunschwig and Fils.
Caramel.

ORIOLE, c.1830.
Brunschwig and Fils. Red
and green on beige.

76

❀ FLEUR DE MAI. French (Alsace), c. 1835, block print. 100% cotton. 53½" wide, 28¾" repeat. Document at Musée des Arts Décoratifs, Paris. No. 61630.01 (cream ground).

❀ FLOREAL GLAZED CHINTZ. French (Alsace), c. 1838, block print. 100% cotton. 48¾" wide, 38¼" repeat. Document at Musée des Arts Décoratifs, Paris. No. 61640.01 (multi).

❀ NANCRAY. English, c. 1830, block and roller print. Lewis, pl. 142. 100% cotton. 54" wide, 14½" repeat. Document in Brunschwig Archives. No. 61518.01 (caramel).

❀ ORIOLE. English, c. 1830, roller print. Montgomery, *Printed Textiles*, fig. 380. 100% cotton, glazed. 48" wide, 15¼" repeat. Document owned by Winterthur Museum. No. 65810.01 (red and green on beige).

❀ PARTERRE. French (Alsace), c. 1835, block print. 100% cotton. 49½" wide, 30¾" repeat. Document at Musée des Arts Décoratifs, Paris. No. 61700.01 (multi).

❀ SCOTLAND GLAZED CHINTZ. French, c. 1820–40, roller print. 100% cotton, glazed. 57" wide, 24" repeat. Document at the Musée de l'Impression sur Etoffes, Mulhouse, France. No. 173880.00 (multi on white).

❀ TREDWELL GARLAND. English, c. 1830–40, block and roller print. 100% cotton. 50¾" wide, 23" repeat. Document in Brunschwig Archives. No. 66388.01 (tea).

FLOREAL GLAZED CHINTZ, c. 1838. Brunschwig and Fils. Multi.

EMILY, c. 1830—45.
Clarence House. Pink and
dark blue; brown and red.

ESSEX LADY SLIPPER,
c. 1835—40. Scalamandré.
Magentas, brown, green,
peach and plum on
off-white.

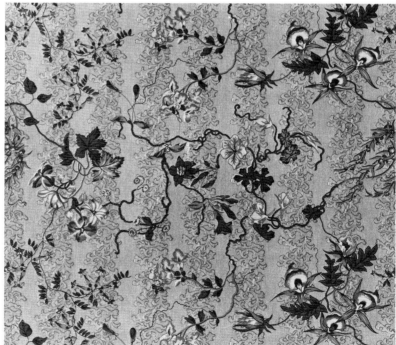

❀ TRILPORT. English or French, c. 1830, block print. 100% cotton. 48″ wide, 23¼″ repeat. Document in Brunschwig Archives. No. 75120.04 (red and blue).

CLARENCE HOUSE

❀ COLETTE. French, c. 1830–40, roller print. 100% cotton, glazed. 54″wide, 17″repeat. Document privately owned in France. No.32097-1 (rose). Minimum order two yards.
❀ EMILY. English, c. 1830–45, block and roller print. 100% cotton, glazed. 53″wide, 14″repeat. Document privately owned in England. No. 32138-1 (pink and dark blue); No. 32138-2 (brown and red). Minimum order two yards.

COWTAN AND TOUT

❀ SEA CORAL. English, c. 1835–50, block print with pin dot ground. 100% cotton, glazed. 51″wide, 4″repeat. Document privately owned in England. No. 6035 (blues on off-white ground); No. 6034 (reds on off-white ground).

DECORATORS WALK

❀ MENDHAM PRINTED CHINTZ. English, c. 1820–40, block print. 100% cotton, glazed. 36″ wide, 21¼″ repeat. Document privately owned. No. T25123 (gold).

I. D. INTERNATIONAL

❀ COMPOSÈ. English, c.1830–40, block and roller print. 100% cotton, glazed. 50″wide, 24½″repeat. Document not located but appears to be an excellent presentation of color and design elements of dark-ground print featuring passion flowers, a design unavailable elsewhere. Printed in Brazil. No.70485-A (green and cordovan).

SCALAMANDRÉ

❀ ESSEX GARDEN. English, c. 1835–45, roller print. 100% cotton. 54″wide, 25¼″repeat. Document at Essex Institute, Salem, Mass. No. 7773-1 (multi on espresso).
❀ ESSEX LADY SLIPPER. English, c. 1835–40, roller print. 100% cotton, glazed. 48″ wide, 16″ repeat. Document at Essex Institute, Salem, Mass. No. 6830-1 (magentas, brown, green, peach and plum on off-white).
❀ LADY OF THE LAKE. French, c. 1830, roller print. 100% cotton. 30½″ wide, 35″ repeat. Reproduced for San Francisco Plantation, Garyville, La. Document privately owned. No. 6426-1 (charcoal on beige). Special order only.
❀ PILLAR. English, c. 1815–30, roller print. 100% cotton, glazed. 50″ wide, 13″repeat. Document at Essex Institute, Salem, Mass. No.7711-1 (multi on brown).

PILLAR, c. 1815–30.
Scalamandré. Multi on
brown.

WILTON HOUSE FLORAL,
c. 1820–40. Scalamandré.
Reds and greens on dark
brown.

SUNNYSIDE LEAF,
c. 1830–45. Schumacher.
Document charcoal.

● WILTON HOUSE FLORAL. English, c. 1820–40, block print. 100% cotton. 49″ wide, 15½″ repeat. Document owned by National Society of the Colonial Dames of America in the State of Virginia. Reproduced for their property Wilton House, Richmond. No. 6364-1 (reds and greens on dark brown).

● WILTON PHOENIX BIRD. English, c. 1820–40, block print. 100% cotton. 47½″ wide, 13″ repeat. Document owned by National Society of the Colonial Dames of America in the State of Virginia. Reproduced for their property Wilton House, Richmond. No. 6349-3 (multi on brown).

SCHUMACHER

● THE QUEEN'S AVIARY. English, c. 1830, block print. 100% cotton, glazed. 54″ wide, 25″ repeat. Document owned by Schumacher. Reproduced with endorsement of The Victorian Society in America. No. 73300 (document multi).

● SUNNYSIDE LEAF. English, c. 1830–45, block print. 100% cotton, glazed. 54″ wide, 1½″ all-over repeat. Document owned by Sleepy Hollow Restorations, Tarrytown, N.Y. No. 72190 (document charcoal).

THE QUEEN'S AVIARY,
c. 1830. Schumacher.
Document multi.

DIANTHUS, c. 1835—45.
Waverly Fabrics. Amber.

WAVERLY FABRICS
OLD STURBRIDGE VILLAGE REPRODUCTIONS

❋ DIANTHUS. English, c. 1835—45, block and roller print. 100% cotton. 54″ wide, 13½″ repeat. Document a whole-cloth quilt in textile collection at Old Sturbridge Village, Sturbridge, Mass. No. 651531 (amber).

WOVEN DESIGNS

BRUNSCHWIG AND FILS

❋ DAVOUT SNOWFLAKE LAMPAS. French, early 19th century. 51% silk, 49% cotton. 48″ wide, 8¼″ repeat. Reproduced for Chillman Empire Parlor, Bayou Bend Collection, Houston. Document in Brunschwig Archives. No. 32261.00 (red); No. 32262.00 (blue); No. 32263.00 (gold); No. 32264.00 (green). Also available as coordinating panel design for chair seat and back and as plain yardage with wide or narrow borders and with coordinating plain satin.

❋ HAMBLEDON WOOL DAMASK. See page 26. This fabric is found on furniture of the period 1815—40 as well as earlier periods.

LAMPAS, c. 1825–40. Scalamandré. Blue and ivory on green.

SCALAMANDRÉ

❋ JULIETTE GORDON LOW DAMASK. French, c. 1815–30. 37% silk, 63% cotton. 51″ wide, 25″ repeat. Document owned by Juliette Gordon Low Birthplace, Savannah. No. 97428-1 (antique gold).

❋ LAMPAS. French, mid-19th century. 100% silk. 49″ wide, 30½″ repeat. Document at Lyndhurst, Tarrytown, N.Y. No. 97124-1 (gold and orange). Special order only.

❋ LAMPAS. French, c. 1825–40. 100% silk. 51″ wide, 48″ repeat. Document owned by Scalamandré. No. 410-1 (blue and ivory on green). Special order only.

❋ XIX CENTURY DAMASK. French, mid-19th-century revival of a mid-18th-century rococo design. 25% silk, 74% cotton. . 51″ wide, 23″ repeat. Document a drapery panel from Sorrel-Weed House, Savannah. No. 97371-1 (old gold on gold).

❋ XIX CENTURY STRIPE. French or English, c. 1830–45. 32% silk, 68% cotton. 53″ wide. Document owned by Sorrel-Weed House, Savannah. No. 99440-1 (beige, rose and charcoal).

1840 TO 1870:
POPULARITY IN FURNISHING FABRICS

In the mid-19th century, the use of textiles to decorate American houses was lavish, reflecting both the availability of a wide variety of fabrics in many price ranges and the interest women took in the appearance of their homes. Fashionable fabrics included silk, velvet, damask, plush, rep, plain satin and figured chintz. Twentieth-century interest in the handsome chintzes of this period has resulted in an abundance of excellent reproductions, but it should be remembered that at the height of fashion in the mid-19th century, chintz was used primarily in bedchambers or as a summer covering.

These years saw the rise of furnishing warehouses in large cities. Such firms employed design consultants and provided furnishings for all aspects of a domestic interior, drapery as well as furniture. A good example is the firm of Leon Marcotte, in New York City, which served clients in every part of the country. Similar firms were established in Boston, New York, Philadelphia, Baltimore, Washington, Cincinnati, Chicago, St. Louis and New Orleans.

Popular magazines and domestic advice books made it possible for those who did not or could not employ professional decorators or upholsterers to make their own fashionable curtains and bed hangings. Advice was even given on ways to create comfortable and fashionable upholstered furniture from packing crates and barrels. Sarah Josepha Hale, in *Godey's Lady's Book,* and Catherine Beecher and Harriet Beecher Stowe, in *The American Woman's Home* (1869), stressed the importance of women's personal involvement in home decorating. Rooms embellished with the products of women's hands were considered symbols of successful attention to domestic duty.

Both Mrs. Hale and the Beecher sisters provided written descriptions and practical illustrations for creating inexpensive but fashionable interiors that fulfilled the ultimate goal — a "homelike" setting. All three authors urged women not to lament their situation but to use their innate talent to create an attractive and welcoming domestic atmosphere at little expense to their husbands. They insisted, for example, that less than a dollar's worth of fabric could be fashioned into handsome curtains, an important component of the domestic interior, which enclosed the family

CACTUS FLOWER, c. 1850–70. Clarence House. Brown and beige.

87

circle and set it aside from the rigors of the workaday world. The influence of these ideas and suggestions can be seen in the middle-class interiors illustrated in Edgar Mayhew and Minor Myers's *A Documentary History of American Interiors* and in William Seale's *The Tasteful Interlude*.

As in previous decades, high-style interior design was characterized by historical revival styles; often different periods were reflected in different rooms within the same house. The basic formula for window curtains remained unchanged—layered curtains, with sheer undercurtains, heavy side draperies and a shaped valance that might be distinctively Greek, Gothic, Moorish or Jacobean. Beginning in 1838, flat, shaped valances stiffened by buckram or paper were introduced, although the complex folds and swags derived from the earlier French drapery style continued in use. The exposed pole with large brass or wooden rings also was still used, as were decorative cornices above concealed curtain rods. The heavy curtain panels were often lined with chintz, sometimes in a color corresponding to or harmonizing with the fabric of the curtain panel but often in beige or tan. The tops of these panels were usually arranged in a series of flat pleats, usually stitched down for two or three inches and bound across the top with tape of some kind. Simple brass hooks were sewn to the back of the pleats; these hooks were then passed through small rings on a pulley device on a concealed rod or at the bottom of the large, exposed rings, which slid freely on decorative curtain poles.

Plain damask, velvet, silk rep and moreen were used for parlor and sitting room curtains, which could be arranged in two or three layers of different color and texture with additional embellishment in braid, fringe, cord and tassels. Tiebacks usually were made of one of these decorative trimmings, almost never of matching fabric. Undercurtains could be sheer cotton muslin, either plain or embellished with embroidery. After the invention of the lace curtain machine in 1849, more and more people selected lace curtain panels for this purpose.

The fashion for heavier fabrics continued to prevail in the treatment of dining rooms and libraries; wool rep and velvet were especially popular for these rooms. Crimson continued to be used extensively in these rooms, and deep olive green was also popular; these dark colors were often enhanced by gold braid and cords.

Samuel J. Dornsife illustrates some specific designs for this period in "Design Sources for Nineteenth-Century Window Hangings"; others are illustrated in William Seale's *The Tasteful Interlude* and in Edgar Mayhew and Minor Myers's *A Documentary History of American Interiors*. Many of these effects can be achieved today by using solid-colored silk, rep, moreen or velvet with an appropriate variety of braids, fringes and trimming. Although few documentary reproductions of these plain materials are available, an excellent selection of appropriate fabrics can be found. Some suggestions are given in the chapter on modern textiles in this book, but do not hesitate to use others. Reproductions of appropriate curtain rods, rings and cornices are much more difficult to find; indeed, they may require custom work. If such accessories are unavailable and no specific design prototype for the situation at hand exists, it might be wise to select a curtain treatment that makes use of a concealed rod.

During the mid-19th century, kitchen curtains began to be used extensively for the first time. They usually were made of simple cotton muslin, checked dimity or dotted swiss. The styles tended to be straight panels with a narrow casing at the top, hung on a rod, wire or string, often covering only the lower half of the window opening.

Dotted swiss and specially made lace panels were used to curtain windows in exterior doors. Roller blinds continued to be popular, the bold transparent landscapes of the earlier decades giving way to more chaste designs of flowers or landscapes in small central medallions or simple gilded moldings.

Bedchambers were decorated in a variety of ways. Colorful printed chintzes were recommended by professional upholsterers and designers, yet some best chambers were fitted up with heavy silk or wool drapery in the styles used in parlors, with bed hangings to correspond. In some homes, dimity continued to be used for bed and window curtains, bedroom slipcovers and toilet table covers.

In this period upholstered furniture became much more dominant in the domestic interior, providing comfort and a sense of luxury unknown in previous generations. Deep spring seats and lavish use of cushions were characteristic. In some cases the upholstery completely overran the furniture frame, reducing it to nothing more than a set of wooden legs supporting fabric-covered cushions.

Plain or patterned horsehair was used extensively for furniture upholstery during this period. Moreen and silk or wool damask were also used. A new fabric was a lightweight twilled wool challis printed in colorful floral designs that could be used for drapery as well as upholstery. "Longfellow House" is a good reproduction of this type of material, the original of which was chosen by Henry Wadsworth Longfellow and his bride, Fanny Appleton Longfellow, for their parlor in Cambridge, Mass., in 1842. Silk was used for the upholstery of some sets of parlor furniture, but it was clearly not the first choice of many people.

This period saw a growing fashion for needlework upholstery or upholstery incorporating embroidered strips or medallions. Such work was a perfect vehicle for personal involvement in the complexity of the fashionable interior, reflecting the ideals of domesticity in a visible and concrete way. Some of the designs for needlework upholstery or upholstery elements were published in sewing manuals or needlework magazines; thus, they may be easily copied today if appropriate materials are selected. Some of the designs were sold as embroidery kits; these may be more difficult to reproduce, especially if they incorporate cut steel beads.

Loose cushions began to be used extensively on sofas, and the number of footstools and ottomans with upholstered tops multiplied as well. In most cases, the fabrics used corresponded with those used on the other upholstered furniture in the rooms, but needleworked designs were chosen for these pieces as well.

Because the variety of designs considered appropriate continued to increase, careful research is the most important element in recreating an accurate interior. Many designs can be easily copied or successfully interpreted in modern materials. The hardest part is selecting designs and fabrics that accurately reflect the tastes and economic situation of the original owner. Persons seeking to achieve an appropriate period effect have a much simpler task, made easier by the fact that the work of interior designers has been studied and published and some of the domestic advice books of this period have been reprinted.

PRINTS

BRUNSCHWIG AND FILS

❀ ANTIBES GLAZED CHINTZ. French (Alsace), c. 1850, block print. 100% cotton, glazed. 65″ wide, 51″ drop repeat. Design by Jean Ulrich Tournier. Document privately owned in France. No. 171470.00 (multi on white).

❀ AUGUSTA GLAZED CHINTZ. English, c. 1850–60, block print. 100% cotton, glazed. 55″ wide, 36″ repeat. Document privately owned in England. No. 66340.01 (cream).

HIDCOTE GLAZED
CHINTZ, c. 1850–60.
Brunschwig and Fils.
Green.

❀ BEAUNE COTTON PRINT. English (for the Portuguese market), c. 1850–60, block and roller print. 100% cotton. 49½″ wide, 14″ repeat. Document privately owned in France. No. 174302.00 (blue).

❀ BETTINA. French, mid-19th century, roller print. 100% cotton. 48" wide, 29¾" drop repeat. Document at Victoria and Albert Museum. No. 37811.01 (red and mauve on cream).

❀ CASHEMIRE COTTON. French (Thierry-Mieg, Mulhouse), 1865, roller print. *Chefs d'Oeuvre du Musée de l'Impression sur Etoffes, Mulhouse,* vol. 1, fig. 99. 100% cotton. 51½" wide, 12½" repeat. Document at Musée de l'Impression sur Etoffes, Mulhouse, France. No. 61251.01 (red).

❀ CHELSEA. English, mid-19th century, roller print. 100% cotton. 49½" wide, 13" repeat. Document at Victoria and Albert Museum. No. 65642.01 (teal).

❀ DONNEYBROOK GLAZED CHINTZ. French (Alsace), c. 1845, block print. 100% cotton, glazed. 52" wide, 40" repeat. Original design by Jean Ulrich Tournier; adapted slightly to make animal elements less ferocious. Document privately owned in France. No. 76917.04 (multi on aubergine).

❀ EBURY. English, c. 1850–70, block print. 100% cotton, glazed. 53" wide, 16" repeat. Document privately owned in England. No. 61601.01 (red).

❀ FILIGREE STRIPE GLAZED CHINTZ. English, c. 1835-45, roller print. 100% cotton, glazed. 53" wide, 31½" repeat. Design slightly enlarged and one motif added. Document owned by Winterthur Museum has a pink ground; another privately owned document has a green ground. No. 65744.01 (green).

❀ HIDCOTE GLAZED CHINTZ. English, c. 1850–60, block print. 100% cotton, glazed. 51" wide, 35" drop repeat. Document privately owned in England. No. 61124.01 (green).

❀ LA FLORE. French, mid-19th century, roller print. 100% cotton. 50" wide, 19⅝" repeat. Document at Musée de l'Impression sur Etoffes, Mulhouse, France. No. 67841.01 (red).

❀ LA PORTUGAISE. English (for the Portuguese market), mid-19th century, block print. 100% cotton, glazed. 50" wide, 34" repeat. Document privately owned in England. No. 172630.00 (multi on aubergine).

❀ MALABAR. French, mid-19th century, roller print. 100% cotton. 48" wide, 18⅝" repeat. Document in Brunschwig Archives. No. 65150.01 (multi on cream).

❀ MOIS DE MAI GLAZED CHINTZ. French (Alsace), c. 1840, block print. 100% cotton, glazed. 50" wide, 31" repeat. Original design by Jean Ulrich Tournier. Document in Brunschwig Archives and at Musée de l'Impression sur Etoffes, Mulhouse, France. No. 61090.01 (white).

❀ MON JARDIN GLAZED CHINTZ. French (Alsace), c. 1850, roller print. *Chefs d'Oeuvre du Musée de l'Impression sur Etoffes, Mulhouse,* vol. 1, fig. 93. 100% cotton, glazed. 63" wide, 38½" repeat. Original design by Jean Ulrich Tournier. Document in Brunschwig Archives and at Musée de l'Impression sur Etoffes, Mulhouse, France. No. 610700.00 (multi on ivory).

✿ POND LILY GLAZED CHINTZ. English, mid-19th century, block print. 100% cotton, glazed. 53½″wide, 35″repeat. Document retained at print works in England. No. 66250.01 (red and green on cream).

✿ ROSES AND LEAVES GLAZED CHINTZ. English, mid-19th century, block print. 100% cotton, glazed. 48½″ wide, 35″ repeat. Hand-blocked. Document privately owned in England. No. 61554.01 (red and emerald).

✿ ROSES AND RIBBONS GLAZED CHINTZ. American, c. 1860, roller print. 100% cotton, glazed. 48″wide, 30″repeat. Original document printed on challis. Document in Brunschwig Archives. No. 77359.04 (green ribbons on charcoal).

✿ ROSES ET LILAC GLAZED CHINTZ. French, mid-19th century, roller print. 100% cotton, glazed. 48″wide, 32¼″ repeat. Document privately owned. No. 37401.01 (pink and blue on off-white).

✿ SAUVIE ISLAND GLAZED CHINTZ BORDER. French or English, c. 1850, roller print. 100% cotton, glazed. 48″wide (composed of 6 border motifs, each 6½″ wide), 6½″ repeat. Reproduced for Bybee-Howell House, Portland, Ore. Document in Brunschwig Archives. No. 77608.04 (brown).

✿ TITANIA GLAZED CHINTZ. French, mid-19th century, block print. 100% cotton, glazed. 52⅛″ wide, 23¾″ repeat. Document in Brunschwig Archives. No. 77560.04 (rose and mauve with blue stripe). Special order only.

✿ VERSAILLES ROSE GLAZED CHINTZ. English, mid-19th century, block print. 100% cotton. 50″wide, 39½″repeat. Handblocked. Document privately owned in England. No. 173950.00 (pink and green on white).

✿ VICTORIAN GARDEN GLAZED CHINTZ. English, c. 1850, block print. 100% cotton, glazed. 50″wide, 30½″half-drop repeat. Document owned by Winterthur Museum. No. 65807.01 (rose and blue on aubergine).

CLARENCE HOUSE

Minimum order two yards.

✿ ACONITE. English, c. 1850–60, roller print. 100% cotton, glazed. 55″ wide, 12″ repeat. Document privately owned in England. No. 32031-1 (violet and brown).

✿ ASQUITH. English, c. 1850–60, block print. 100% cotton, glazed. 52″ wide, 13¼″ repeat. Document owned by Clarence House. No. 32087-3 (taupe); No. 32087-5 (blue).

✿ BAILEY ROSE. English, c. 1850–70, block print. 100% cotton, glazed. 53″wide, 39″repeat. Document owned by Clarence House. No. 31925-1 (pink).

✿ BRAGANZA. English (for the Portuguese market), c. 1850–60, block and roller print. 100% cotton. 52″wide, 14″repeat. Document privately owned in England. No. 32128-1 (midblue).

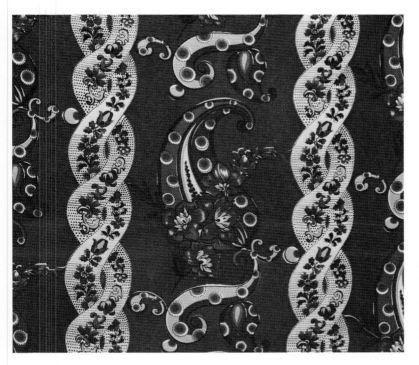

BRAGANZA, c. 1850–60.
Clarence House. Midblue.

VICTORIAN GARDEN
GLAZED CHINTZ, c. 1850.
Brunschwig and Fils. Rose
and blue on aubergine.

FRAGONARD, c. 1850—65.
Clarence House. Rose.

❂ CACTUS FLOWER. English, c. 1850—70, block and roller print. 100% cotton, glazed. 53″ wide, 14″ repeat. Document privately owned in England. No. 32126-1 (brown and beige).

❂ EUGENIE. English, c. 1860—75, block and roller print. 100% cotton, glazed. 52″ wide, 31″ repeat. Document privately owned in England. No. 32033-1 (red and green).

❂ FRAGONARD. English, c. 1850—65, block print. 100% cotton, glazed. 56″ wide, 26½″ repeat. Document owned by Clarence House. No. 32089-1 (rose).

❂ GALLICA. English, c. 1845—60, block and roller print. 100% cotton, glazed. 52″ wide, 26″ repeat. Document privately owned in England. No. 32066-1 (red and turquoise).

❂ LA VEILLE VARSOVIE. English, c. 1850—70, block print. 100% cotton, glazed. 41½″ wide plus 7½″ border on one side, 28¾″ repeat. Original document on wool ground. Document owned by Clarence House. No. 31987-101 (aubergine).

❂ LIBERTY ROSE CHINTZ. English, c. 1850—70, block print with fancy ground. 100% cotton, glazed. 50″ wide, 14½″ repeat. Document privately owned. No. 32002-1 (multi).

❂ L'OPERA CHINOIS. English, c. 1850—70, block print. 100% cotton. 51″ wide, 15″ repeat. Document owned by Clarence House. No. 31929-61 (ecru, unglazed); No. 31929-1 (ecru, glazed).

❂ MELBOURNE. English, c. 1850—70, block print. 100% cotton,

glazed. 54″wide, 18″repeat. Document privately owned. No. 7349-5C (red and teal).

❀ MUSSET. French, c.1845—70, block print. 100% cotton, glazed. 51″ wide, 30¼″ repeat. Document privately owned. No. 32015-1 (creme).

❀ NOAILLES. English, c. 1850—70, block print. 100% cotton, glazed. 58″ wide, 25½″ repeat. Document privately owned. No. 32074-2 (celadon).

❀ OLD ROSE. English, c. 1845—70, block print. 100% cotton, glazed. 50″ wide, 17½″ repeat. Document privately owned in England. No. 31745-1 (rose and cream).

❀ ROPE LATTICE. English, c. 1860, block print. 100% cotton, glazed. 48″ wide, 24″ repeat. Document owned by Clarence House. No. 2505178 (creme); No. 2552855 (green).

❀ ROSA MUNDIE. English, c. 1850—65, block print. 100% cotton, glazed. 54½″ wide, 21½″ repeat. Document privately owned in England. No. 32032-2 (blue).

❀ ROSE CUMMING CHINTZ. English, c.1850—65, block print. 100% cotton, glazed. 51″wide, 35½″repeat. Document privately owned. No. 31410-01 (multi on ice blue).

❀ ROSE SPRIG. English, c.1840—50, block and roller print. 100% cotton, glazed. 52″ wide, 13″ repeat. Document privately owned. No. 32067-1 (turquoise).

❀ TREE POPPY. English, c. 1850—65, block and roller print. 100% cotton, glazed. 52″wide, 29″repeat. Document privately owned in England. No. 32130-1 (red and green).

COWTAN AND TOUT

Minimum order two yards.

❀ ALEXANDRA CHINTZ. English, c. 1840—50, block and roller print. 100% cotton, glazed. 54″wide, 18″repeat. Document owned by Cowtan and Tout. No. 6422 (reds and greens on beige ground).

❀ BAILEY ROSE. English, c. 1860—90, block print. 100% cotton, glazed. 50″ wide, 38″ repeat. Document owned by Cowtan and Tout. No. 7180 (reds, pinks and greens on white ground).

❀ CROCUSES. English, c. 1845—65, block with pin dot ground. 100% cotton, glazed. 54″wide, 3½″repeat. Document owned by Cowtan and Tout. No. 4100 (pinks and blue on white ground).

❀ DIANTHUS. English, c. 1850—65, block print with fancy ground. 100% cotton, glazed. 54″wide, 11″repeat. Document privately owned in England. No. 1350 (reds and blues on cream ground).

❀ FLORAL BOUQUET AND RIBBON. English, c. 1860—1900, block print. 100% cotton, glazed. 53″ wide, 39″ repeat. Document privately owned in England. No. 2033 (reds, pinks and greens on ivory ground).

❀ PEARL STRIPE AND RIBBON. English, c. 1860—70, block print. 100% cotton, glazed. 52″wide, 25″repeat. Document owned by Cowtan and Tout. No. 5054 (pink and white with green stripes).

TREE POPPY, c. 1850–65.
Clarence House. Red and
green.

HOLLYHOCK PRINT,
c. 1850–60. Lee Jofa.
White, reds and turquoise.

❀ ROSE AND LABURNUM. English, c. 1845–60, block print with squiggle ground. 100% cotton, glazed. 50″wide, 29″repeat. Document owned by Cowtan and Tout. No. 7040 (reds and lilac on fancy squiggle ground).

❀ VICTORIA. English, c. 1860–80, block print. 100% cotton, glazed. 50″wide, 18″repeat. Document owned by Cowtan and Tout. No. 9701 (rose and green with blue stripes on white ground).

❀ WINDSOR ROSE. English, c. 1860–90, block print. 100% cotton, glazed. 54″wide, 35½″repeat. Document owned by Cowtan and Tout. No. 82000-1 (reds and greens on white ground); No. 82000-2 (reds and greens on blue ground).

FONTHILL

❀ LILAS. English, c. 1855–70, block print. 100% cotton, glazed. 62″ wide, 45″ repeat. Document owned by Fonthill. No. 1533-6 (green ground).

GREEFF FABRICS

❀ CANTERBURY HILL. English, c. 1840–60, block print. 100% cotton, glazed. 56″wide, 16″repeat. Document privately owned in England. No. 60646 (rose and blue on mocha).

❀ HATFIELD. English, c. 1850–70, block print with fancy ground. 100% cotton, glazed. 50″wide, 30″repeat. Document owned by Greeff. No. 54670 (lilac and rose on natural).

❀ HATHAWAY HOUSE. English, c. 1860, block print. 100% cotton. 36″wide, 16″repeat. Document privately owned in England. No. 55835 (red).

❀ KENDRICK. English, c. 1860, block print. 100% cotton, glazed. 56″ wide, 36″repeat. Document privately owned in England. No. 60873 (old rose and lilac on ivory).

I. D. INTERNATIONAL

❀ IMPERIAL GATE. 100% cotton, glazed. 50″wide, 4½″repeat. Document not located; contains printed Gothic elements unavailable elsewhere. No. 20991 (forest green). Minimum order three yards.

LEE JOFA

❀ GRANVILLE PRINT. English, c. 1860, block print. 100% cotton, glazed. 54″ wide, 29½″ repeat. Document owned by Lee Jofa. No. 789030 (multi on cream).

❀ HOLLYHOCK AND RIBBON PRINT. English, c. 1850–75, block print. 100% cotton, glazed. 49-50″ wide, 36″half-drop repeat (cut by repeat only). Document privately owned. No. 799820 (ivory).

❀ HOLLYHOCK MINOR. English, c. 1850–60, block and roller print. 100% cotton, glazed. 52″wide, 23½″repeat. Document owned by Lee Jofa. No. 9395-0 (green, rose and spruce).

LEAVES PRINT, c. 1850.
Lee Jofa. Rose on buff.

❋ HOLLYHOCK PRINT. English, c. 1850–60, block print. 100% cotton, glazed. 47″wide, 40¼″repeat (cut by repeat only). Handblocked. Document privately owned in England. No. 7131 (white, reds and turquoise).

❋ LEAVES PRINT. English, c. 1850, block print. 100% cotton, glazed. 52″wide, 36½″repeat. Document privately owned. No. 809201 (rose on buff).

❋ LUDLOW PRINT. English, c. 1850–60, block print. 100% cotton, glazed. 48-49″wide, 24½″half-drop repeat. Document privately owned in England. No. 789010 (multi on cream); No. 789011 (multi on white).

❋ PORCELAIN FLOWERS PRINT. English, c. 1850–60, block print. 100% cotton, glazed. 50″wide, 27¾″repeat. Handblocked. Document privately owned in England. No. 99348 (white, red and turquoise).

❋ ROSEBANK PRINT. English, c. 1850–60, block print. 100% cotton, glazed. 49-50″wide, 36″repeat. Document privately owned in England. No. 789000 (white and red).

❋ ROSEDALE PRINT. English, c. 1860, block print. 100% cotton, glazed. 50″ wide, 24″ repeat. Document privately owned in England. No. 659080 (red and white).

❋ TRENTHAM HALL PRINT. English, c. 1850–60, block print. 100% cotton, glazed. 53″ wide, 36″ half-drop repeat. Document privately owned in England. Recently converted from handblocked print to rotary screen. No. 647205 (beige and multi).

LUDLOW PRINT,
c. 1850–60. Lee Jofa.
Multi on cream; multi on
white.

ROSEBANK PRINT,
c. 1850–60. Lee Jofa.
White and red.

ROSEDALE PRINT, c. 1860.
Lee Jofa. Red and white.

WHIPPETS PRINT,
c. 1850–60. Lee Jofa.
Multi on cream.

SWAN LAKE, c. 1845–55.
Scalamandré. Charcoal,
greens and red.

❋ WHIPPETS PRINT. English, c. 1850–60, block print. 100% cotton, glazed. 53-54″ wide, 25¼″ repeat. Adapted slightly to make animal elements less ferocious. Document owned by Lee Jofa. No. 769040 (multi on cream).

ROSE CUMMING CHINTZES

No order numbers; use name of design.

❋ CLIMBING GERANIUM. English, c. 1840–60, block print with vermicelli ground. 100% cotton, glazed. 50″ wide, 16″ repeat. Document privately owned. Rose and dark green on cream.

❋ LILAC. French, continuous from c. 1860, block print on striped pin-dot ground. 100% cotton. 46″ wide, 37″ repeat. Example is owned by Society for the Preservation of New England Antiquities, Boston. Creme.

❋ MARLBOROUGH. English, c. 1855–80, block print with fancy ground. 100% cotton, glazed. 50″ wide, 22″ repeat. Document privately owned in England. Rose and green on white.

❋ PELARGONIUM FANCY. English, c. 1840–70, block print with vermicelli ground. 100% cotton, glazed. 51″ wide, 34″ repeat. Document privately owned. Rose and green on cream.

SCALAMANDRÉ

❋ LONGFELLOW HOUSE. English, c. 1840, printed wool. 100% wool twill. 55″ wide, 10¼″ repeat. Document a printed wool fabric purchased in 1842 by Henry Wadsworth Longfellow and Fanny Appleton Longfellow from James Paul and Company of Boston; used for window drapery

102

CHATEAU SUR MER, c. 1854. Schumacher. Document gold.

and furniture upholstery in their parlor in Cambridge, Mass. Document owned by Longfellow National Historic Site. No. 7793 (multi on beige). Adaptation on 100% cotton, glazed. No. 7795 (multi on beige).

❈ SWAN LAKE. English, c. 1845–55, roller print. 100% cotton. 50" wide, 14" repeat. Document at Essex Institute, Salem, Mass. No. 6277-4 (charcoal, greens and red).

SCHUMACHER

Asterisk after a catalog entry denotes fabric produced with the endorsement of the Victorian Society in America.

❈ CHATEAU SUR MER. French or English, c. 1854, silk brocade. 97% cotton, 3% other fiber. 54" wide, 27" repeat. Document a silk brocade provided by New York City firm of Leon Marcotte in 1854 for drapery and furniture upholstery in ballroom of Chateau sur Mer, Newport, R.I. Document owned by Preservation Society of Newport County. Adapted to a screen print on cotton rep. Reproduced for Chateau sur Mer. No. 75990 (document gold).

❈ FERNDALE. Probably English, c. 1850, printed wool. 50% rayon, 37% cotton, 13% wool. 48" wide, 28½" repeat. Document owned by Cooper-Hewitt Museum. No. 73370 (document multi).*

❈ GRANDE BAROQUE. Probably English, c. 1860, printed wool. 100% cotton. 48" wide, 25" repeat. Document owned by Cooper-Hewitt Museum. No. 73400 (document brown).*

❈ LOTTIE'S LACE. Probably English, c. 1840–50, cylinder print. 100% cotton, glazed. 54" wide, 8¼" repeat. Document owned by Cooper-Hewitt Museum. No. 73410 (coral and green).*

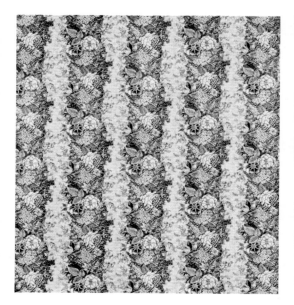

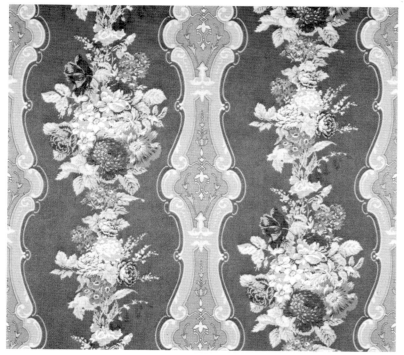

top left
LOTTIE'S LACE,
c. 1840–50. Schumacher.
Coral and green.

top right
VICTORIA AND ALBERT
CHINTZ,
1854. Stroheim
and Romann. Red on
white.

right
GRANDE BAROQUE,
c. 1860. Schumacher.
Document brown.

VICTORIA DAMASK,
c. 1840. Brunschwig and
Fils. Pink.

STROHEIM AND ROMANN

❀ VICTORIA AND ALBERT CHINTZ. English, 1854, block print. 100% cotton. 50″ wide, 31″ repeat. Designed for the first royal yacht of Queen Victoria; design contains profiles of Victoria and Albert. Document privately owned in England. No. 34370 (red on white).

WAVERLY FABRICS
OLD STURBRIDGE VILLAGE REPRODUCTIONS

❀ AUSTIN. English, c. 1840–55, roller print. 100% cotton, glazed. 54″ wide, 27″ repeat. Document in textile collection of Old Sturbridge Village, Sturbridge, Mass. No. 687731 (beige and red).

WOVEN DESIGNS

BRUNSCHWIG AND FILS

❀ MARCOTTE DAMASK. French, 19th century. 100% silk. 48″ wide, 19½″ repeat. Reproduced for American Wing, Metropolitan Museum of Art. Special order only.
❀ ROANNE SILK DAMASK. European, mid-19th century. 100% silk. 48″ wide, 19½″ repeat (cut by repeat only). Reproduced for Belter Parlor (1845–70), Bayou Bend Collection, Houston. Document in Brunschwig Archives. No. 31620.00 (vieux rose, No. 7009).
❀ VICTORIA DAMASK. English, c. 1840. 58% cotton, 30% wool, 12% rayon. 51″ wide, 20″ repeat. Document is wool draperies from a Virginia plantation; now at Valentine Museum, Richmond. No. 10705.02 (pink).

OLD WORLD WEAVERS

❀ BROCATELLO MUSEO. Probably Italian, mid-19th century. 96% silk, 4% linen. 50″ wide, 3¾″ repeat. Reproduced for American Wing, Metropolitan Museum of Art. No. A2474 (royal blue and gold).

LEE JOFA

❀ SCOTTISH TARTANS. Traditional. 100% wool. 54″ wide, repeats vary. Clans available:
HUNTING MACINTOSH. No. 4634-0.
BLACK WATCH. No. 4636-0 (blue and green).
HUNTING MENZIES. No. 4638-0 (red and green).
GREEN BARCLAY. No. 4639-0 (navy and green).
MUTED RED HUNTING CHISHOLM. No. 4640-0 (brown, light blue, red).
BLACK WATCH MUTED. No. 4641-0 (gray and mink).
LINDSAY. No. 4643-0 (maroon and green).
RED MACINTOSH. No. 4644-0 (red and navy).
DRESS STEWART. No. 4645-0 (white and multi).
MUTED HUNTING STEWART. No. 4647-0 (brown).
HUNTING CHISHOLM. No. 4648-0 (brown and green).
ANDERSON. No. 4710-0.

CLAN CAMERON. No. 4712-1.
HUNTING FRASER. No. 4713-1.
KENNEDY. No. 4714-1.
HUNTING MACLEOD. No. 4715-1.
DRESS MENZIES. No. 4716-1.
PRINCESS MARY. No. 4718-1.
GREEN DOUGLAS. No. 4719-1.
BROWN SCOT. No. 4720-1.
ANCIENT MACMILLAN. No. 4722-1.
ANCIENT CAMPBELL. No. 4723-1.
ELLIOTT. No. 4724-1.
DARK JOHNSTON. No. 4725-1.
DRESS MACDUFF. No. 4727-1.
HUNTING MACINNES. No. 4728-1.
MACLENNAN. No. 4729-1.
ANCIENT HUNTING MACRAE. No. 4730-1.
WALLACE. No. 4731-1.
GREY DOUGLAS. No. 4732-1.
HUNTING MACPHERSON. No. 4733-1.
ANDERSON MUTED. No. 4734-1.
DOUGLAS MUTED. No. 4735-1.
MACKELLAR MUTED. No. 4736-1.
HUNTING MACINTOSH MUTED. No. 4737-1.
DRESS MACKENSIE MUTED. No. 4738-1.
PRINCESS MARY MUTED. No. 4740-1.

❀ WYMONDHAM DAMASK. English, c. 1845–70. 56.5% cotton, 43.5% silk. Document privately owned in England. No. K211-3. Special order only; colors to order.

SCALAMANDRÉ

❀ BALLROOM SATIN. c. 1855–70. 42% silk, 58% cotton. 50½" wide. Suitable texture for formal drapery and upholstery. Document owned by Scalamandré. No. 99450-4 (kelly green).

❀ LOUIS XVI LAMPAS. c. 1855–75. 65% silk, 35% cotton. 50" wide, 26¾" repeat. Document owned by Scalamandré. No. 586-12 (gold and silver on royal blue). Special order only.

❀ MUSEUM OF THE CITY OF NEW YORK DAMASK. c. 1870. 100% silk. 51" wide, 9" repeat. Reproduced for Rockefeller Room, Museum of the City of New York. Document owned by Scalamandré. No. 97201-1 (cardinal red). Special order only.

❀ PATRICK BARRY BROCATELLE. c. 1850–65. 65% silk, 35% linen. 50" wide, 26½" repeat. Document owned by Scalamandré. No. 97120-1 (bronze, french gray and white).

❀ STAN HYWET BROCATELLE. c. 1850–70. 36% silk, 64% linen. 50" wide, 27¾" repeat. Document owned by Scalamandré. No. 97321-1 (slate blue strié).

107

1870 TO 1900:
NEW INFLUENCES AND VARIETY

M any American houses during the years 1870–1900 were characterized by heavy window drapery and luxurious upholstery, lavish ornaments and abundant use of table covers, lambrequins and purely decorative textile accents. The fabrics used included richly textured brocatelle, brocade, lampas and damask; delicate shades of soft silk and satin; elaborately patterned cretonne, cashmere and tapestry; and highly polished chintz. During the summer months, many of these heavy decorative elements were carefully stored away and replaced by lighter window curtains, rush mats and rugs and brightly colored chintz slipcovers.

Throughout the period solid-colored window curtains were still popular for primary rooms. Complex decorative effects were achieved through the use of many layers of fabric and contrasting colors and trims. These elaborate window curtain designs were set off nicely by the crisp white muslin or lace curtains used next to the window panes and the window shades beneath them.

The heavy winter window hangings were often made of solid-colored wool or velvet panels trimmed with decorative woven tapes or bands of embroidery. Damask and moreen were also used. The curtains were usually surmounted by decorative lambrequins and cornices and further set off by elaborate fringes, tassels and tiebacks. Because of the elaborate folds in window curtains, stiff rep was used less frequently than in the previous decades.

For simpler houses, one or more of these layers might be omitted and less expensive fabrics and trimmings substituted. Some of the cheaper fabrics could be made to simulate those of richer texture by the use of extra lining and interlining. As a substitute for costly trimmings, attractive decorative accents could be made at home. One author suggested using gray linen damask curtain panels bordered with embroidered flowers or figures cut from scarlet, blue or green cloth and appliqued to the linen. Figures cut from chintz or cretonne could also be used to embellish simple curtains. One author even suggested gluing bands of colorful autumn leaves to strips of muslin and using these as curtain borders, adding a thin tree branch as a cornice. This combination was thought to create a truly medieval appearance and could be expected to last at least one season.

NAPOLEON TROIS, c. 1870–90. Brunschwig and Fils. Multi on green trellis.

In addition to window drapery, additional interior embellishment was introduced in the form of portieres, which were interior curtains hung in doorways. These could be hung from thick wooden rods on exposed rings or above the door frame on an apparatus concealed by an elaborate lambrequin. Closely woven fabrics, such as wool rep, were favored for portieres as the most effective means of stopping drafts between rooms. In many cases portieres were trimmed with horizontal bands of appliqued velvet or embroidery, the placement of which could reflect the architectural divisions of the adjacent walls. Less commonly, the portieres matched the window drapery within a room.

Decorating conventions dictated appropriate colors for the various rooms in a house. Parlors should be opulent, adorned with the most expensive fabrics in jewellike colors, while family sitting rooms were to be furnished with colorful chintz and cretonne in luxurious shades of blue, drab, gray or pale rose. Libraries and dining rooms were still decorated in more somber colors such as brown, stone, dark green, crimson or dull red; wool, damask and velvet were the fabrics considered especially well suited to these rooms.

Bed chambers could be decorated in silks and damasks as rich as those used in parlors, but many people favored lighter effects achieved with cretonne, sateen, cashmere or chintz in brighter colors and more lively prints. Beds were once again hung with elaborate drapery, although seldom with fully enclosing curtains. Light and airy netted canopies were introduced during this period as a decorative covering for old high-post bedsteads. Even simple brass beds were adorned with curtains hung from a rod or boxed frame fixed to the wall above the headboard.

In the late 19th century, many people changed their interior decor seasonally, packing away heavy window drapery, portieres and table covers to protect them from moths and making way for light-colored, gaily patterned, washable fabric furnishings. Light or white ground chintzes on cretonnes in bright floral prints were highly favored, although those with buff or blue grounds were also used. In some houses, ruffled swiss muslin or dotted swiss cotton was used for window curtains, slipcovers, dressing tables and bed drapery. If color was desired, the white cotton could be lined with a chintz of a bright, contrasting color or embellished by colored ribbons drawn through broad hems or used as informal tiebacks. Summer textiles might be made of simpler fabrics, but they were not necessarily used in simple ways. In *Beautiful Homes* (1878), Henry T. Williams and Mrs. C. S. Jones proclaimed that "exquisite puffs and neatly fluted ruffles" in abundance were still the order of the day.

Lace curtains could be used year-round, alone in summertime and covered by heavy and colorful curtains in winter. In selecting Nottingham lace curtains, people were advised to choose those of a soft, yellowish cream color rather than those of glaring bleached white. Small-figured designs and delicate motifs were recommended, among them fine fern sprays, conventional flowers, ivy sprays and imitations of old laces.

Roller blinds or window shades of buff holland were similarly chosen for the warm color they gave to the light passing through them. However, some people thought that white cotton or linen shades harmonized better with other drapery and upholstery, and they had the further advantage of being easier to launder. Painted window shades continued to be used, although the brilliant transparent landscapes gave way to solid-colored panels of ivory, gray or lavender embellished with gilded panels with corner scrolls or a single central motif of a vase of fruit or flowers. On some of the more expensive shades, these ornamental elements might be highlighted with mica.

Several books and many articles in popular periodicals gave precise instructions for fashionable drapery and upholstery. Anyone attempting to recreate an interior of this period should survey the contemporary magazines. The books written by Henry T. Williams and Mrs. C.S. Jones, such as *Beautiful Homes* (1878), are especially well illustrated, highly descriptive and practical.

Throughout these years, ornamental needlework was extensively used in curtain and upholstery borders and accents and on decorative accessories such as cushions, lamp rugs, footstools, lambrequins, mantel drapery, table covers, doilies, antimacassars and wall pockets. Patterns for such items were published in all the popular ladies' magazines and individual books of instruction as well. Needlework kits with designs prestamped on appropriate fabrics and the colors of the embroidery silks or wools charted could be purchased. For modern reproduction of these accessories and trimmings, see Sophia Caulfeild and Blanche Saward's *The Dictionary of Needlework* (1882) or *The Lady's Handbook of Fancy Needlework* (1880), both of which have been recently reprinted. For a different point of view, see Constance Cary Harrison's *Women's Handiwork in Modern Homes* (1881) or the various works of Candace Wheeler.

Throughout the late 19th century, the design and use of furnishing fabrics reflected several new influences. The design reform movement produced advocates, practitioners and publications as well as the distinctive flat-patterned fabrics in the style of William Morris.

The Morris-style fabrics seem to have a special appeal to the late 20th-century eye and have been reproduced by several companies. Bear in mind that these fabrics were not widely distributed in their own time. They were expensive, handprinted textiles sold through a few interior design firms, such as A.H. Davenport of Boston. They usually were used in highly structured interiors, not highlighted in flat panels as examples of fine design.

At the same time, there was a revival of American colonial and Federal period motifs and a few early reproductions of 18th-century French "toiles." Some of the reproductions of 18th-century copperplate-printed fabrics, particularly the French ones listed earlier in this book, may be useful for persons trying to create the appearance of the early Colonial Revival. Simple ruffled muslin curtains were used in bedchambers of this style; in some New England houses, they were even used in parlors. These curtains were known as "Priscillas," an allusion to Longfellow's heroine thought to make them seem more antique. Like the netted bed canopies and hooked rugs that were part of the same style, these curtains were new elements crafted to give the appearance of simplicity and great age.

During the 1880s exotic interests resulted in a distinct but fairly short-lived passion for Japanese designs. Only a few reproductions that reflect this taste are available, but suitable effects can be achieved with plain fabrics and appropriate design and trimming.

The late 19th century also saw a move toward classicism in high-style interior decoration, explained most fully in Edith Wharton and Ogden Codman's book *The Decoration of Houses* (1897). This text suggests treating windows in a distinguished architectural way rather than concealing them with elaborate drapery; personal comfort should override lush and opulent upholstery. Wharton and Codman advocate the use of muslin curtains only as a transparent screen intended to provide privacy in an interior. They denounced the currently popular lace curtains as an obstruction of the exterior view and an attempt to show off the luxury of the interior to passersby.

Despite the best efforts of the reformers, American popular taste continued to favor lavish textile furnishings in domestic interiors. This taste is well documented in the illustrations then published in *Harper's Weekly*, as sheet music covers or as accompaniment to contemporary fiction. Current fascination with the period has produced many useful compendia of period photographs, among them Nicholas Cooper's *The Opulent Eye*, William Seale's *The Tasteful Interlude* and a number of regional studies.

In recent years, interiors of the period 1870–1900 have received increasing attention from preservationists and restorers. As a result, many more documentary reproduction fabrics for this period have been made available in the past six years. Bear in mind, however, that most of these have been commissioned for specific restorations. Although for the most part they are well done, they do not necessarily represent the most typical fabrics available at that time; they are more a reflection of modern circumstances than period taste. Careful research may dictate that none of these fabrics is appropriate for a particular restoration project. Fortunately, many late 19th-century designs can be recreated from solid-colored fabrics of suitable texture combined with appropriate trimmings. In some cases, however, custom reproduction may still be necessary.

PRINTS

BRUNSCHWIG AND FILS

❊ CHENIER WARP PRINT ON TAFFETAS. French, c. 1880–1900. 100% silk. 51″ wide, 20½″ repeat. Document privately owned in France. No. 39420.00 (cream ground).

❊ CHURCHILL COTTON AND LINEN PRINT. English, c. 1870–1900,

block print. 46% cotton, 54% flax. 47″ wide, 9¼″ repeat. Document privately owned in England. No. 66358.01 (nutmeg leaf).

❀ DR. THORNTON'S TULIPS. English, c. 1880–1900, roller print. 100% cotton, glazed. 48″ wide, 21″ repeat. Document in Brunschwig Archives. No. 76248.04 (green, brown and cream).

❀ GRENELLE PRINTED TAFFETA. French, c. 1880–1900, block print. 100% silk. 48″ wide, 24½″ repeat. Document privately owned in France. No. 35650.00 (cream ground).

❀ LES PAPILLONS EXOTIQUES. French, c. 1885–1900, roller print. 100% cotton. 51″ wide, 17″ repeat. Document privately owned. No. 173418.00 (multi on brown).

❀ NAPOLEON TROIS. French, c. 1870–90, roller print. 100% cotton. 50″ wide, 24″ half-drop repeat. Document privately owned in France. No. 66334.01 (multi on green trellis).

❀ NARCISSUS. American, c. 1885–90, block print. 100% cotton. 54″ wide, 15½″ repeat. Original design by Candace Wheeler. Adaptation of 100% linen original. No. 72264.04 (green, yellow and white). Available in 100% linen by special order.

CLARENCE HOUSE

❀ PENELOPE. English, block print, c. 1870–90. 100% cotton, glazed. 48″ wide, 20″ repeat. Document privately owned in England. No. 32068-1 (lilac and pink).

NARCISSUS, c. 1885–90. Brunschwig and Fils. Green, yellow and white.

BROTHER RABBIT, 1882.
Scalamandré. Wine red on
off-white.

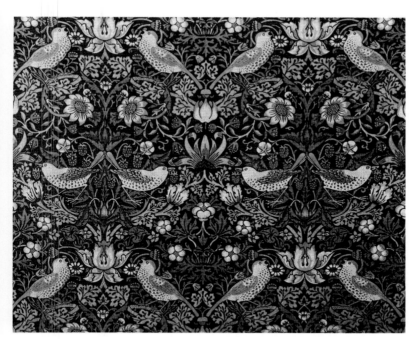

STRAWBERRY THIEF,
1883. Scalamandré. Light
blue, pink, yellow and
moss green on deep blue.

DAFFODIL, c.1891.
Scalamandré. Greens,
pink, yellow and rust on
off-white.

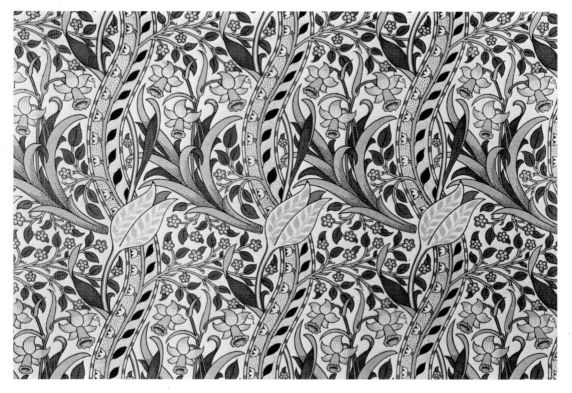

❀ RUBENS. French, c. 1880–1900, block print. 100% cotton, glazed. 51"wide, 47"repeat. Document privately owned in France. No. 31777-2 (cream); No. 31777-12 (cream; 60% linen, 40% cotton).

COWTAN AND TOUT

❀ BOUQUET AND LATTICE. English, c. 1880–1900, block print. 100% cotton, softly glazed. 50"wide, 19½"repeat. Document privately owned. No. 4403 (rose and greens on white ground).

❀ GLYNDEBOURNE. English, c. 1880–1900, block print. 100% cotton, glazed. 54" wide, 27" repeat. Document privately owned. No. 5666-7 (lilac and rose on white ground).

❀ HANDBLOCKED LILY AND AURICULA. English, c. 1880–1900, block print. 100% cotton, glazed. 48"wide, 32"repeat. Handblocked. Document privately owned in England. No. 5045 (red, beige and white on aqua ground).

LEE JOFA

❀ BALMORAL PRINT. English, c. 1890–1900, block print. 100% cotton, glazed. 49-50"wide, 19½"repeat. Document owned by Lee Jofa. No. 789203 (mauve, pink and aquarelle).

SCALAMANDRÉ

❀ BROTHER RABBIT. English, 1882, block print. Clark, no. 14. 100% cotton. 49½"wide, 12½"repeat. Original design by William Morris. Document owned by North American Branch of the William Morris Society. No. 6785-1 (wine red on off-white).

❀ DAFFODIL. English, c. 1891, block print. Clark, no. 37. 100% cotton. 48"wide, 12¾"repeat. Original design by William Morris (his last chintz design). Document owned by North American Branch of the William Morris Society. No. 6794-1 (greens, pink, yellow and rust on off-white).

❀ LODDON. English, 1884, block print. Clark, no. 29. 100% cotton. 48"wide, 19³⁄₁₆"repeat. Original design by William Morris. Document owned by North American Branch of the William Morris Society. No. 6802-1 (light blue, pinks, yellow and olive green on beige). See cover.

❀ MERRIMACK VALLEY FLORAL. American (Cocheco Mills, Dover, N.H.), 1887, roller print. 100% cotton. 54"wide, 18"repeat. Originally printed on cretonne; now printed on sateen. Document owned by Marrimack Valley Textile Museum, North Andover, Mass. No. 7778-1 (multi on cream).

❀ STRAWBERRY THIEF. English, 1883, block print. Clark, no. 22. 100% cotton. 49"wide, 19⁷⁄₁₆"repeat. Original design by William Morris; the first successful indigo discharge printing by Morris at Merton Abbey. Document owned by North American Branch of the William Morris Society. No. 6792-1 (light blue, pink, yellow and moss green on deep blue).

MERRIMACK VALLEY FLORAL, 1887. Scalamandré. Multi on cream.

✵ VANDERBILT MANSION BLUE ROOM. French, c. 1896, roller print. 56% cotton, 44% linen. 50" wide, 26" repeat. Document a printed version of an 18th-century silk brocade used in 1896 in Blue Room of Vanderbilt Mansion National Historic Site, Hyde Park, N.Y. No. 6818-1 (roses, oranges, greens and tans on beige).

✵ WILLOWY FIELDS. English or American, c. 1890, block print. 100% cotton, glazed. 48" wide, 27" repeat. Document privately owned. No. 6809-4 (multi on eggshell).

SCHUMACHER

✵ GERTRUDE'S BOUQUET. English, c. 1895, block print. 100% cotton, glazed. 54" wide, 18" repeat. From an original cretonne selected by Ogden Codman for Gertrude Vanderbilt Whitney's bedroom at The Breakers, Newport, R.I. Document owned by Preservation Society of Newport County. No. 75M970 (document rose).

✵ LILY. English, c. 1890, block print. 100% cotton, glazed. 54" wide, 6⅝" repeat. Document an original design by Arthur Wilcock owned by Cooper-Hewitt Museum. No. 73380 (document brown).

✵ MUSICAL GARLANDS. English or American, c. 1895, block print. 100% cotton. 48½" wide, 28" repeat. From an original cretonne selected by Ogden Codman for Gertrude Vanderbilt Whitney's dressing room walls and curtains at The Breakers, Newport, R.I. Document owned by Preservation Society of Newport County. No. 75M940 (document rose and green).

MONTEGO BAY DAMASK,
c.1870–95. Scalamandré.
Cream on ming gold.

❁ PAINTED TAPESTRY. English, c.1895. 52% linen, 48% cotton. 54″ wide, 13½″ repeat. From an original silk and linen textile chosen by Ogden Codman for Mrs. Cornelius Vanderbilt's bedroom walls at The Breakers, Newport, R.I. Document owned by Preservation Society of Newport County. No.75M930 (document rose).

❁ RIBBON FLORAL. English or French, c. 1895, block print. 100% cotton, glazed. 54″wide, 14″repeat. From an original chintz selected by Ogden Codman for The Breakers, Newport, R.I. Document owned by Preservation Society of Newport County. No. 75M980 (document rose).

❁ VANDERBILT FLORAL. French or English, c.1895, block print. 100% cotton, glazed. 46″wide, 36″repeat. From an original chintz selected by Ogden Codman for Gertrude Vanderbilt Whitney's bedroom walls at The Breakers, Newport, R.I. Document owned by Preservation Society

118

of Newport County. No. 75M950 (document rose and green).

❋ WHITNEY FLORAL. French or English, c. 1895, block print. 100% cotton. 54″ wide, 28″ repeat. From an original cretonne selected by Ogden Codman for Gertrude Vanderbilt Whitney's bedroom at The Breakers, Newport, R.I. Document owned by Preservation Society of Newport County. No. 75M960 (document rose).

DECORATORS WALK

WOVEN DESIGNS

In addition to the fabrics listed here, Decorators Walk has many other late 19th-century revivals of 18th-century silk lampas and brocade designs that are suitable for this period.

❋ BUCKINGHAM PALACE LINEN DAMASK. Low Countries, c. 1870–1900. 100% linen. 56″ wide, 27″ repeat. Revival of an early 18th-century design. Document privately owned. No. L58690 (natural). Special order only.

❋ JACOBEAN LINEN DAMASK. Low Countries, c. 1870–1900. 100% linen. 56″ wide, 27″ repeat. Revival of a 17th-century design. Document privately owned. No. L58260 (natural). Special order only.

❋ LINEN DAMASK. Low Countries, c. 1870–1900. 100% linen. 56″ wide, 18¾″ repeat. Revival of an early 18th-century design. Document privately owned. No. L27820 (natural).

❋ MEDICI LINEN DAMASK. Low Countries, c. 1870–1900. 100% linen. 56″ wide, 27″ repeat. Revival of a 17th-century design. Document privately owned. No. L58100 (natural).

❋ PALAIS LISERE. French, c. 1880–1900. 78% cotton, 22% spun rayon. 49″ wide, 29⅛″ repeat. Revival of an 18th-century design. Document privately owned. No. T31568 (multi on white).

SCALAMANDRÉ

❋ 1890 HOUSE DAMASK. French or Italian, c. 1890–1900. 23% silk, 77% cotton. 51″ wide, 20″ repeat. Document owned by Scalamandré. No. 97405-6 (banana).

❋ HONOLULU JASPÉ SATIN. Country of origin unknown, c. 1880–84. 44% silk, 56% cotton. 50″ wide. Document at Iolani Palace, Honolulu. No. 99464-1 (wine).

❋ IOLANI BROCATELLE. Country of origin unknown, 1884. 46% silk, 54% linen. 48½″ wide, 18″ repeat. Document provided by A.H. Davenport of Boston for the Throne Room Chairs at Iolani Palace, Honolulu. Document owned by Iolani Palace. No. 97395-1 (red).

❋ MONTEGO BAY DAMASK. Probably French or Italian, c. 1870–95. 100% silk. 50½″ wide, 62″ repeat (cut by repeat only). Document owned by Scalamandré. No. 97178-2 (cream on ming gold).

❋ VANDERBILT. Country of origin unknown, c. 1890–1900. 35% silk, 65% cotton. 50½″ wide. Document owned by Vanderbilt Mansion National Historic Site, Hyde Park, N.Y. No. 97429-1 (aqua and pale yellow).

MODERN TEXTILES:
CONTINUING A TRADITION

S ome modern textiles that have changed little or not at all from the originals of an earlier date are entirely appropriate for restoration work. Sources for some of these fabrics—including plain-woven checks, cottons and linens, baize, diaper, dimity, plush, rep and horsehair — are provided in the following sections. The fabrics listed here are intended only as an elementary guideline to the identification of appropriate fabrics or a shortcut to ordering suitable goods. Because many similar fabrics are available in retail shops throughout the country, feel free to search elsewhere for traditional fabrics that are still being manufactured or for those that visually resemble the products of an earlier time. While purists may wish to use natural fibers exclusively for restoration work, in some cases compromise on this point can result in visual similarity at greatly reduced cost.

THE DORR MILL STORE
❀ RUG WOOL. 100% wool. 60" wide. No. 1313 (green); No. 6307 (dark blue); 32 other colors available.

SCALAMANDRÉ
❀ INDEPENDENCE HALL BAIZE CLOTH. No. 99243. (See page 26).
❀ SHELBOURNE CASEMENT. 50% wool, 50% cotton. 50" wide. No. 99412-1 (white). Also available in 5 colors. Dyed width 47". Consider especially No. 99412-5 (bottle green).

SUNFLOWER STUDIO
❀ CARPET BAIZE. 100% wool. 36" wide. A heavy weight especially suitable for crumb cloths. Handwoven. No. X18.12 (cream white). Can be dyed to order; 35 colors available, including 7 shades of green.
❀ FLANNEL BAIZE. 100% wool. 36" wide. A lighter weight more appropriate for table coverings and quilt tops. Handwoven. No. C14.11 (cream white). Can be dyed to order; 35 colors available, including 7 shades of green.

BAIZE

COLONIAL CHECK LINEN. Sunflower Studio. Indigo blue and cream white.

121

BORDERINGS

During the period 1750–1800, some bed and window valances were made with applied borders of printed fabric. These were constructed of strips cut from yard goods, the raw edges of which were folded under and the resulting piece of fabric applied to the edge of the valance. The raw edges of the valance itself were folded up "to the right side" and completely covered with the appliqued strip of cloth. This treatment gave a neatly finished look to the valance, providing no visible hems, a clean finish on the inside and a well-defined outline to the shaped valance on the outside. In this period, some fabrics were intentionally printed in a series of stripes with broad areas between them so that the stripes could be cut apart and used for borderings. Not everyone used these specific fabrics for this purpose, however, and there are numerous examples of valances bordered with strips of printed cotton of all-over design. "Williamsburg Liner Stripe" is an excellent reproduction of the type of bordering specially printed in this style. The other fabrics listed here are nondocumentary prints that are considered especially appropriate for this use.

BRUNSCHWIG AND FILS

❀ CORALITO COTTON PRINT. 100% cotton. 51″ wide, 9″ repeat. No. 173852.00 (blue); other colors available.
❀ PEAWEED COTTON PRINT. 100% cotton. 48″ wide, 3½″ repeat. No. 66201.01 (raspberry); other colors available.

COWTAN AND TOUT

❀ SQUIGGLE CHINTZ. 100% cotton, glazed. 54″ wide, 4″ repeat. No. 5607 (green on cream ground); other colors available. Minimum order 2 yards.

SCHUMACHER
COLONIAL WILLIAMSBURG REPRODUCTION

❀ WILLIAMSBURG LINER STRIPE. English, c. 1750–80, block print. Montgomery, *Printed Textiles,* figs. 2 and 428 (top). 100% cotton. 50″ wide, 1″ repeat. Document owned by New York Historical Society, New York City. No. 63113 (document red).

CHECKS

Plain-woven checks and simple plaids have changed little in the last 200 years. The tabby woven patterns of regular or irregular repeats of squares were relatively easy to establish on hand looms, and a surprising variety of decorative effects was achieved within this basic design formula. From the earliest days of settlement in America, checks were used for clothing as well as for bed and window curtains and loose cases or slipcovers for furniture. The earliest examples of checks were all linen, and although they could be made on home looms, they were also imported in enormous quantities. Checks and stripes were among the first products of American cotton textile mills, and these fabrics, too, were used in household decoration as well as for more utilitarian items such as mattress and pillow

COUNTRY CHECK LINEN. Sunflower Studio. Indigo blue and cream white.

ticking in addition to clothing. To judge from surviving examples dating before the mid-19th century, blue and white was the most common color combination, although red, green and various shades of gold and brown were also combined with white. Sometimes the gold or brown was combined with blue as well as white. Until the mid-19th century, the texture of cotton check was somewhat heavier than that of modern gingham, and the heavier checks seem to have always been preferred for household furnishings; indeed, they have often been referred to as "furniture checks." Many textile firms carry checks as part of their regular stock. In addition, some museum reproduction checks are available:

BRUNSCHWIG AND FILS

❁ ANGLET CHECK. 100% cotton. 50″wide, ⅞″repeat. No.64220.01 (beige and brown).
❁ BELLAC CHECK. 47% cotton, 37% viscose rayon, 16% linen. 55″ wide, ¾″repeat. No.69968.01 (tan and blue).

CRANSTON PLAID.
Waverly Fabrics. Indigo.

❀ BUTTERSCOTCH WOVEN PLAID. Pennsylvania, c. 1775–1825. 85% viscose, 15% linen. 54″ wide, 1¼″ repeat. Adapted from a woven cotton-and-linen check at Winterthur Museum. No. 60516.01 (butterscotch and blue).

❀ ISIGNY CHECK. 47% cotton, 37% rayon, 16% linen. 55″ wide, 2″ repeat. No. 140442.00 (navy).

❀ POTOMAC LINEN CHECK. 62% linen, 38% cotton. 54″ wide, 3″ repeat. No. 69051.01 (red on cream); No. 69052.01 (blue on cream).

SCHUMACHER
COLONIAL WILLIAMSBURG REPRODUCTIONS

Documents are in the textile collection of Colonial Williamsburg, Williamsburg, Va.

❀ EDINBURGH CHECK. 100% linen. 48″ wide, 2″ repeat. No. 83174 (blue).

❀ WILLIAMSBURG CHECK. 18th or early 19th century. 55% linen, 45% cotton. 48″ wide, ½″ regular squares. No. 118880 series.

❀ WILLIAMSBURG TAVERN CHECK. 61% linen, 39% cotton. 48″ wide, 3″ squares. Document an 18th-century linen case for a settee cushion. No. 81508 (document blue).

SUNFLOWER STUDIO

❀ COLONIAL CHECK LINEN. 100% linen. 30″ wide, 2″ repeat. No. C7.1 (indigo blue and cream white only). Handwoven.

❀ COUNTRY CHECK LINEN. 100% linen. 30″ wide, 1″ check, 2″ repeat. No. B6.1 (indigo blue and cream white only). Handwoven.

❀ LINSEY-WOOLSEY CHECK. 82% linen, 18% wool. 30″ wide, 1″ repeat. No. D8.1 (available in 35 colors, each with white). Handwoven.

❀ VILLAGE CHECK LINEN. 100% linen. 30″ wide, ⅜″ repeat. No. C5.1 (indigo blue and cream white only). Handwoven.

WAVERLY FABRICS
OLD STURBRIDGE VILLAGE REPRODUCTIONS

Documents are in the textile collection of Old Sturbridge Village, Sturbridge, Mass.

❀ CRANSTON CHECK. 59% Dacron polyester, 41% cotton. 54″ wide, ¾″ repeat. Document an early 19th-century handwoven linen apron. No. 645702 (indigo).

❀ CRANSTON PLAID. 100% cotton. 54″ wide, 1½″ repeat. Document an early 19th-century cotton bolster cover. No. 645692 (indigo).

❀ TOWNE CHECK. 100% cotton. 54″ wide, ⅜″ repeat. Document an early 19th-century cotton handkerchief. No. 602230 (butternut).

BRUNSCHWIG AND FILS

CHINTZ

❀ ALBI PLAIN GLAZED CHINTZ. 100% cotton. 50″ wide. No. 6569.01 (103 colors).

❋ MAJA FIGURED CHINTZ. 100% cotton, glazed. 50″ wide. No. 6571.01 (80 colors).

CLARENCE HOUSE
❋ PARIS CHINTZ. 100% cotton, glazed. 52″ wide. No. 32726 (65 colors).

FONTHILL
❋ GLAZED CHINTZ. 50% cotton, 50% polyester. 48″ wide. No numbers; order by name only (19 colors).
❋ MOIRE STRIPE. 100% cotton, glazed. 54″ wide, 2″ repeat. No. 1540-5 (green); No. 1540-2 (scarlet).

GREEFF FABRICS
❋ CAROUSEL GLAZED CHINTZ. 100% cotton. 50″ wide. No. 126280 (25 colors).

I. D. INTERNATIONAL
❋ COTTON CHINTZ. 50% cotton, 50% Dacron, glazed. 48″ wide. No numbers; order by name (20 colors).
❋ CHINTZ. 50% cotton, 50% polyester, glazed. 48″ wide. No. B. Berger 2101 (50 colors).

LEE JOFA
❋ CHINTZ CAMILLE. 100% cotton, glazed. 51″ wide. No. 824300 series (34 colors).
❋ CHINTZ MALMAISON. 100% cotton, glazed. 51″ wide. No. 794500 series (41 colors).

SCALAMANDRÉ
❋ CHICA CHINTZ. 50% cotton, 50% Dacron, glazed. 48″ wide. No. 99738 series (13 colors).
❋ PARIS SPRING. 100% cotton, glazed. 48½″ wide. No. 98189 series (19 colors).

COTTONS

Plain-woven cottons and synthetic-cotton blends of good texture are available from a number of manufacturers listed in this book as well as in drapery and clothing fabric shops throughout the country. Some examples suitable for restoration work are listed here:

BRUNSCHWIG AND FILS
❋ ORGANDY COTTON. 100% cotton (preshrunk). 43″ wide. No. 8556.02 (white).

E. C. CARTER, GREEFF FABRICS
❋ COTTON BATISTE. 100% cotton. 44″ wide. No. 30474 (white).

❋ DOTTED SWISS. 50% cotton, 50% Kodel polyester. 44″wide. No. 30483 (white).

❋ EMBROIDERED BATISTE. This firm specializes in embroidered batiste designs. More than 60 designs are available, some of them in colors on white. Many of these are suitable for late 19th-century restoration work. Some appropriate for any date in the 19th century are:
No. 33975, 65% Dacron, 35% cotton. 45″wide, 2″repeat. White. Sold in 15-yard pieces.
No. 33750, a design of two sizes of white dots embroidered on white. 65% Dacron, 35% cotton. 44-45″wide, 3″repeat. White.
Consider also Nos. 34070, 33935, 34125, 33945 and 34135.

❋ EMBROIDERED DOTTED BATISTE. 65% Dacron, 35% cotton. 43″wide, 2″repeat. No. 30534 (white).

❋ EMBROIDERED STRIPED BATISTE. 65% Dacron, 35% cotton. 45″ wide. No. 33620 (white).

❋ EYELET EMBROIDERED BATISTE. 65% Dacron, 35% cotton. 45″ wide, 2″repeat. No. 34130 (white on white).

❋ ORGANDY. 100% cotton. 44″wide. No. 30106 (white).

❋ VERTICAL STRIPED DOTTED SWISS. 50% cotton, 50% polyester. 44-45″wide. No. 1500 (white).

DECORATORS WALK

❋ BATISTE. 100% polyester. 47-48″wide. No. HC81660 (white); No. 81661 (oyster).

❋ BATISTE II. 100% polyester. 48″wide. No. HC76552 (oyster); No. 76550 (white).

❋ BROADCLOTH. 65% polyester, 35% cotton. 45″ wide. No. HC78497 (white).

❋ COTTON BATISTE. 100% cotton. 45″ wide. No. HC78495 (white).

❋ COTTON VOILE. 100% cotton. 50″wide. No. HC79250 (white).

❋ DOTTED SWISS. 65% polyester, 35% cotton. 45″ wide. No. HC70590 (white).

❋ EMBROIDERED BATISTE. 65% polyester, 35% cotton. 43″ wide. No. HC80065 (white).

❋ MARQUISETTE. 100% polyester. 118″wide. No. HC70311 (white); No. HC70312 (eggshell). 114″wide, No. HC74420 (white).

❋ ORGANDY. 100% cotton. 44″wide. No. HC79255 (white).

❋ PERMANENT FINISH ORGANDY. 100% cotton. 42-43″wide. No. HC77049 (white).

❋ POPLIN CLOTH. 100% cotton. 56″wide. No. IS399-1 (oyster).

❋ SWISS LAWN. 100% cotton. 51″wide. No. Q2949 (white).

❋ VERTI CRASH. 80% polyester, 20% cotton. 48″ wide. No. HC81579 (bone); 4 other colors available.

❋ WOVEN DOTTED SWISS. 65% polyester, 35% cotton. 45″ wide. No. HC 78470 (white).

GREEFF FABRICS
❋ OLYMPIA. 100% cotton. 54" wide. A woven herringbone design. No. 126524 (linen); No. 126525 (mocha).

LEE JOFA
❋ VOILE. 100% cotton. 36"wide. No. 3020 (white).

SCALAMANDRÉ
❋ FRENCH VOILE. 100% cotton. 52"wide. No. 4213-0 (white).
❋ SUMMER NET VOILE. 100% cotton. 55" wide. No. 98235-1 (white).

DIAPER

In the 18th and early 19th centuries in the United States, "diaper" referred to patterned woven cottons and linens that were often used for table linens, napkins and toweling. Rarely is evidence found of their having been used for curtains. These designs can easily be copied by handweavers using published drafts. An excellent selection is given in the two books by Constance Dann Gallagher.

SCALAMANDRÉ
❋ CAMEO CLOTH. 100% cotton. 50"wide. No. 97711-1 (white).

SCHUMACHER
COLONIAL WILLIAMSBURG REPRODUCTIONS
❋ M AND O CLOTH. 100% cotton. 48"wide. No. 84580 (natural).
❋ WILLIAMSBURG DOBBY WEAVE. 100% cotton. 54" wide. No. 81710 (series); 28 colors available.

DIMITY

In the 18th and early 19th centuries, dimity was a heavy cotton cloth distinguished by various patterns of vertical ribs, either regular or irregular. Dimity was used for bed curtains, window curtains, counterpanes, dressing or toilet table covers and slipcovers or loose cases for seating furniture (often called "furniture dimities"). By the late 1820s, dimity was also made in a lighter version that was used mainly for clothing; this was usually referred to as "cap dimity" or "checked dimity," to distinguish it from the heavier furniture dimity. The new fabric also used woven ribs as its primary design characteristic, but the cloth was much lighter in weight and the ribs were spaced more regularly in small stripes or checks. Both dimities were available from about 1825 until the end of the 19th century. In the last quarter of the 19th century, the lighter type of dimity began to be used for curtains in kitchens, bedchambers and summer cottages. Curtains made of lightweight dimity were used extensively in late 19th- and early 20th-century Colonial Revival interiors, although the fabric was unknown in the 18th century. It eventually superceded the heavier furniture dimity and has never gone out of production. Lightweight 100% cotton dimity is difficult to find today, but cotton-polyester blends are available in many department and fabric stores. Available styles of the heavier furniture dimity are listed below.

All dimities can be washed, but those made of 100% cotton will shrink. It is wise to wash a sample yard before cutting the fabric; then measure it and make the necessary allowances when cutting unwashed cloth. Furniture dimity will shrink in length an inch or more per yard. Because of the nature of the woven vertical ribbing in furniture dimity, the horizontal shrinkage will be much greater, as much as 7 inches per yard. This amount can be reduced somewhat by vigorous ironing, which also reduces the characteristically puffy vertical ribs of the freshly laundered fabric.

BRUNSCHWIG AND FILS
❀ NEW RICHMOND DIMITY. 100% cotton. 46½″ wide. No. 69400.01 (white).

SCALAMANDRÉ
❀ BETSY ROSS DIMITY. 100% cotton. 52″ wide. No. 98246-1 (white).
❀ DIMITY. 100% cotton. 50″ wide. No. 1657-1 (colonial white).
❀ DIMITY. 100% cotton. 50″ wide. No. 1658-1 (colonial white).

EMBOSSING

Brunschwig and Fils, Clarence House, Old World Weavers and Scalamandré can emboss designs using 19th-century rollers. Several hundred patterns are available, and selections can be made from illustrated catalogs in the showrooms. Embossed designs are particularly effective on plush or velvet; they can also be used on some silks and wool moreens.

FUSTIAN

SUNFLOWER STUDIO
❀ DOUBLE FUSTIAN. 56% linen (warp), 44% cotton (weft). 30″ wide. Handwoven. No. D1.1 (cream white); No. E1.1 (35 colors available).
❀ JEAN FUSTIAN. 65% linen (warp), 35% cotton (weft). 30″ wide. Handwoven. No. C1.2 (cream white or dyed; 35 colors available).

HORSEHAIR

Beginning in the mid-18th century, plain and patterned horsehair fabrics in black, green, red and white were used for upholstery. Colonial Williamsburg and the Connecticut Historical Society have mid-18th-century examples with a satin woven stripe alternating with a ribbed stripe. Documents of plain satin weave and various diaper woven designs can be dated as early as the late 18th century. All of these styles continued to be made for the next hundred or more years; special medallions for chair seats and sofa upholstery were also made during the 19th century. Authentic horsehair fabrics and accurate reproductions are made with a cotton or linen warp, the weft being made of actual tail or mane hair. The width of the fabric is thus limited by the length of the horsehair, usually from 25 to 30 inches. Nylon imitations of horsehair are usually made wider. A variety of horsehair patterns is currently available; almost all of them are imported. Bear in mind that cuttings or loan samples are seldom available and that orders of horsehair fabrics are apt to have a long delivery time. When ordering horsehair fabric in solid colors, expect some variation in colors because of the natural variation in the way the hair may absorb the dye.

BRUNSCHWIG AND FILS

❋ CHAMFORT HORSEHAIR TEXTURE. A woven design of alternating octagons and diamonds. 60% horsehair, 40% cotton. 27″ wide, 2″ repeat. No. 190279.00 (black); No. 190274.00 (dark green).

❋ CHRISTIANE HORSEHAIR TEXTURE. A woven design of alternating octagons and diamonds. 60% horsehair and hemp, 40% cotton. 27″ wide, 1½″ repeat. No. 190021.00 (red); No. 190028.00 (brown and gold).

❋ CORDAY HORSEHAIR TEXTURE. A woven design with diamonds in a contrasting color. 30% cotton, 30% horsehair, 40% hemp. 27″ wide, ¾″ repeat. No. 190282.00 (blue and gold); No. 190289.00 (black); 5 other colors available.

❋ PALOMINO HORSEHAIR TEXTURE. A woven design of circles alternating with diaper diamonds. 40% cotton, 60% horsehair. 27″ wide, 2″ repeat. No. 190399.00 (black).

❋ RAINCY HORSEHAIR TEXTURE. A satin weave. 60% horsehair, 40% cotton. 27″ wide. No. 180274.00 (green); No. 180278.00 (brown).

❋ SALINS HORSEHAIR TEXTURE. A satin weave. 40% cotton, 60% horsehair. 27″ wide. No. 180599.00 (black).

CLARENCE HOUSE

❋ HORSEHAIR. 50% horsehair, 50% hemp. 25″ wide. No. 1500 series (33 patterns and color combinations currently available).

DECORATORS WALK

❋ HORSEHAIR. 50% cotton, 50% horsehair. 16″ to 27″ wide. 7 patterns and various color combinations; also nylon imitations, which are wider.

LEE JOFA

❋ HORSEHAIR DAMASK. 68% horsehair, 32% cotton. 24″ wide; can be ordered 26-27″ wide for a slight additional charge.

No. 664225. A small diamond diaper design. Red and black.

No. 664226. A woven pattern of alternating octagons and diamonds. 2″ repeat. Blue. Also No. 664227 (green).

No. 664228. A woven pattern of small diaper blocks on a strié ground. 2″ repeat. Gold.

No. 664229. A woven pattern of smaller diaper blocks on a solid ground. 1″ repeat. Black.

No. 664230. A woven pattern of irregularly repeating satin and ribbed

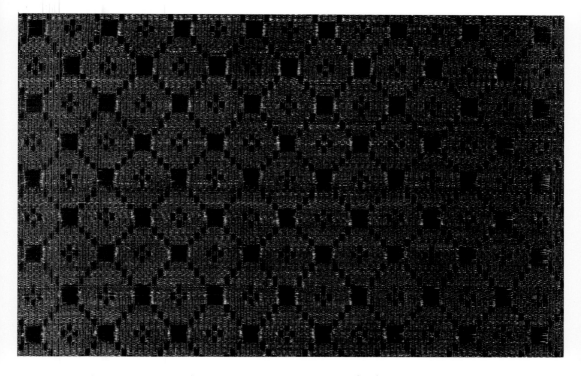

stripes, closely resembling a document, c. 1796, on one of Thomas Jefferson's chairs at Monticello. Black.

🏵 HORSEHAIR SATEENS. 68% horsehair, 32% cotton. 24″ wide, can be ordered 26-27″ wide for a slight additional charge. No. 664238 (black).

OLD WORLD WEAVERS

Offers a variety of ribbed, patterned and striped horsehairs in several colors as well as black.

SCALAMANDRÉ

🏵 HORSEHAIR DAMASK. 60% horsehair, 40% cotton. 26″wide, ¾″ repeat. No. 96409-1 (black).

🏵 HORSEHAIR REPP. 60% horsehair, 40% cotton. 26″ wide. No. 98208-2 (green warp with black hair).

🏵 HORSEHAIR SATEEN DOCUMENT TEXTURE. 60% horsehair, 40% cotton. 26″wide. No. 98207-1 (grays).

🏵 LA FRANCE HORSEHAIR DOCUMENT. 40% cotton, 60% horsehair. 27″wide. A woven diaper design of small diamonds. No. 98164-1 (black).

🏵 NINETEENTH-CENTURY HORSEHAIR DOCUMENT. A satin weave. 60% horsehair, 40% cotton. 26″wide. No. 98206-1 (black).

HORSEHAIR DAMASK.
Scalamandré. Black.

LACE AND NET

Sheer white undercurtains are essential for a successful layered window treatment for any period after about 1820. Although plain cotton batiste (called mull or muslin in the period) was used throughout the 19th century, machine-made embroideries became popular after about 1835 and machine-made lace panels after about 1850. No documentary reproductions of these are available, but some firms carry "traditional" yardage or panels that are appropriate. Some of these designs were introduced fairly soon after machine-made laces were introduced and have never gone out of production; others have been revived recently using traditional technology.

DECORATORS WALK
✱ BOBBINET. Used for a mosquito bar in the restoration of San Francisco Plantation, Garyville, La.; also appropriate for late 19th-century window curtains. 100% polyester. No. HC74660, 70″ wide, white. No. HC74662, 70″ wide, ecru. No. HC69221, 136-140″ wide, white. No. HC69223, 136-140″ wide, ecru.

✱ FERNERY. 100% polyester. 47″ wide, 26¼″ repeat. No. 77116 (eggshell); No. 77117 (snow); No. 77118 (cream).

✱ LACE CURTAINS. 70% polyester, 30% cotton. 57″ wide, 98″ long. No. HC78690 (eggshell). Sold in pairs only.

✱ LACE ELEGANCE. 100% cotton. 60″ wide, 34½″ repeat. No. HC80000 (champagne).

✱ LACE NET. 100% polyester. 118″ wide (can be used either horizontally or vertically). No. HC74721 (white).

✱ POINTE DE SPRIT. 100% polyester. 112″ wide (can be used either horizontally or vertically). No. HC81425 (white); No. HC81426 (eggshell).

✱ STARFLAKE LACE. 70% polyester, 30% cotton. 47″ wide, 7¼″ repeat. No. T34456 (ecru).

✱ VICTORIAN I LACE PANEL. 70% polyester, 30% cotton. 95″ wide, 118″ long. No. HC78790 (champagne). Sold in pairs only; can be ordered twice this width.

✱ VICTORIAN II LACE PANEL. 70% polyester, 30% cotton. 66″ wide, 118″ long. No. HC78795 (champagne). Sold in pairs only; can be ordered twice this width.

✱ VICTORIAN III LACE PANEL. 70% polyester, 30% cotton. 95″ wide, 118″ long. No. HC78785 (champagne). Sold in pairs only; can be ordered twice this width.

✱ WHITE TAMBOUR NET CURTAINS. 100% polyester bobbinet with batiste applique. 44″ wide, 3 yards long. No. HC77092 (white). Sold in pairs only; can be ordered twice this width.

GREEFF FABRICS
✱ AVIARY LACE. 100% cotton. 70″ wide, 3½ yards long. No. 400900 (ivory).

❋ FAIRLIE. 100% cotton. 48"wide, 19"repeat. No. 32495 (ivory).

❋ HURLFORD. 100% cotton. 48"wide, 29"repeat. No. 32490 (ivory).

❋ IVORY BIRDS PANEL. 100% cotton. 59" wide, 106" repeat. No. 401015 (ivory).

❋ KENSINGTON LACE. 100% cotton. 68" wide, 36" repeat. No. 39800 (ivory).

❋ KIRKMICHAEL. 100% cotton. 48"wide. No. 32500 (ivory).

❋ NOTTINGHAM LACE. 85% cotton, 15% polyester. 48" wide, 2" repeat. No. 400840 (ecru).

❋ NOTTINGHAM LACE NET. 100% cotton. 48" wide. Ivory or eggshell. No. 38720, No. 38724; No. 38712; No. 399303; No. 39306; No. 39300; No. 400110; No. 39552, No. 39554; No. 39553; No. 38981; No. 38980; No. 39308; No. 38977.

❋ ROYAL PEACOCK PANEL. 100% cotton. 59"wide, 126"long. No. 401020 (ivory). Sold in pairs only; can be ordered twice this width.

❋ SPANISH LACES. 80% Dacron acrylic, 20% polyester. 48" wide, 15¼"repeat. No. 40121 (white).

LEE JOFA

❋ EDWARD LACE. 100% cotton. 55"wide, 5" repeat. No. 823010 (bone).

❋ ROSEBUD LACE. 100% cotton. 59"wide, 13"repeat. No. 803010 (off-white).

❋ TOMASINA LACE. 100% cotton. 55"wide, 15"repeat. No. 82300 (bone).

SCALAMANDRÉ

❋ EGYPT LACE PANEL. 100% cotton. 60"wide, 126"repeat. Document (c. 1870–90) privately owned in England. No. 96432-1 (off-white).

❋ VICTORIAN WINDOW. 100% cotton. 24"wide, 51"long. Document a late 19th-century Nottingham lace panel window shade privately owned in England. No. 96430-1 (off-white).

STROHEIM AND ROMANN

LEATHER

❋ WINTERTHUR LEATHER. Available in full and half hides. Reproduced for Winterthur Museum. No. 01390 (Essex Room green); No. 01391 (Marlboro Room red); No. 01392 (Tappahanock Room brown); No. 01393 (Wentworth Room brown); No. 01395 (Lancaster Room black); No. 01396 (Centreville Room brown).

BRUNSCHWIG AND FILS

LINENS

❋ GENT LINEN CASEMENT. 64% linen, 25% cotton, 11% rayon. 48"wide. No. 69410.01 (white); No. 69419.01 (eggshell).

❋ SPA PLAIN LINEN. 55% linen, 45% cotton. 50" wide. No. 51059.01 (white); No. 51059.02 (natural).

133

DECORATORS WALK

❈ HANDKERCHIEF LINEN. 100% linen. 46″ wide. No. HC4850 (white). Other linen samples available on request.

SCHUMACHER
COLONIAL WILLIAMSBURG REPRODUCTIONS

❈ TAFFETA LINEN. 100% linen. 50″ wide. Document a linen bed-sheet in textile collection of Colonial Williamsburg, Williamsburg, Va. No. 113887 (natural).

❈ WILLIAMSBURG LINEN STRIPE. 55% linen, 45% cotton. 48″ wide, 1″ horizontal repeat. Document in textile collection of Colonial Williamsburg, Williamsburg, Va. No. 86M551 (biscuit).

SUNFLOWER STUDIO

❈ CANVAS LINEN. 100% linen. 30″ wide. Handwoven. No. B3.4 (cream white); No. C3.4 (35 colors available).

❈ LINEN DRILL. 100% linen. 30″ wide. Twill. Handwoven. No. C1.3 (cream white); No. D1.3 (35 colors available).

❈ PURE LINEN. 100% linen. 30″ wide. Handwoven. No. B3.2 (cream white); No. C3.2 (35 colors available).

❈ TOWCLOTH. 100% linen. 30″ wide. Woven of 50% flax line and 50% tow. Handwoven. No. A4.2 (natural brown only).

HAMILTON-ADAMS
ULSTER WEAVING COMPANY

Both Hamilton-Adams and Ulster stock dozens of types of linen in a variety of colors, textures, widths and weaves, including fine cambrics. Ulster even has 1-inch-wide tabby woven linen tape. The best procedure is to write describing what is wanted and to request samples and a price list. Small yardages are available at a premium price, but the variety and quality are almost impossible to find elsewhere.

LINSEY-WOOLSEY

Despite its extreme popularity as a romantic symbol of frugal, home-spun America, linsey-woolsey was actually not a common fabric in the early years of this country. For those whose documentation requires it, one good source is:

SUNFLOWER STUDIO

❈ HEAVYWEIGHT LINSEY-WOOLSEY. 50% linen, 50% wool. 30″ wide. Handwoven. No. A4.1 (cream white); 35 additional colors available.

❈ LIGHTWEIGHT LINSEY-WOOLSEY. 50% linen, 50% wool. 30″ wide. Handwoven. No. B3.1 (cream white); 35 additional colors available.

❈ LINSEY-WOOLSEY TWILL. 50% linen, 50% wool. 30″ wide. Handwoven. No. C1.4 (cream white); 35 additional colors available.

Marseilles weaves are adaptations of late 18th and early 19th-century machine-woven bed coverings. In many ways these are not appropriate for restoration use because individual design elements have been taken from units composed as large rectangles and have been rearranged to create continuous yardage. They are listed here only as suggestions for use in certain high-traffic or low-budget projects where a handmade reproduction of a white bedcovering cannot be obtained.

MARSEILLES WEAVES

BRUNSCHWIG AND FILS
❀ BEDFORD QUILT. 100% cotton. 50″ wide, 10½″ repeat. No. 80650.02 (bleached white).
❀ BENETTA COTTON MATELASSÉ. 100% cotton. 54″ wide, 9″ repeat. No. 82010.02 (white).
❀ MARCH BANK COTTON MATELASSÉ. 100% cotton. 54″ wide, 13″ repeat. Adapted from a textile document at Winterthur Museum. No. 8202.02 (natural).

AMAZON VINEGAR AND PICKLING WORKS DRYGOODS
❀ OSNABURG. 100% cotton. 44-45″ wide (natural).

OSNABURG

SUNFLOWER STUDIO
❀ BROWN OSNABURG. 100% linen. 30″ wide. Handwoven. No. B3.3 (natural brown).

Although no documentary museum reproductions of plush are currently available, one can safely use any densely woven wool or mohair velvet with a deep pile, preferably at least ³⁄₁₆ inch or ¼ inch. Plush can also be embossed (see note under Embossing). Good examples of plush can be found at Brunschwig and Fils, Clarence House, Decorators Walk, Old World Weavers and Scalamandré.

PLUSH

BRUNSCHWIG AND FILS
❀ DOMMEL MOHAIR VELVET. 38% mohair, 62% cotton. 51″ wide. No. 3612.01 series (22 colors available).

CLARENCE HOUSE
❀ VELOURS MOHAIR. 64% mohair, 36% cotton. 50″ wide. No. 10379 (33 colors).

DECORATORS WALK
❀ DENSEPILE PLUSH. 52% mohair, 24% cotton, 24% polynosic (100% mohair pile). 50″ wide. No. IS1100 series (36 colors).
❀ MOHAIR PLUSH. 60% mohair, 40% cotton (100% mohair pile on 100% cotton back). 54″ wide. No. T34100 series (36 colors).
❀ WOOL PLUSH. 50% cotton, 50% wool. 50″ wide. No. T38555–38574 (20 colors).

❉ WOOL PLUSH. 50% wool, 50% rayon face, 100% cotton back. 54″ wide. No. T40390–40428 (38 colors).

❉ WOOL PLUSH. 100% wool pile, 100% cotton back. 55″ wide. No. T41266–41270 (5 colors).

LEE JOFA

❉ MOHAIR VELOUR. 61% cotton, 39% mohair (100% mohair pile on a 100% cotton back). 50″ wide. No. 805120 series (14 colors).

OLD WORLD WEAVERS

❉ PLUSH. 75% mohair, 25% cotton. 50″ wide. No. J-11229-C (colors to order).

SCALAMANDRÉ

❉ BARONS PLUSH. 47% wool, 53% cotton. 51″ wide. No. 98633 series (16 colors); additional special colors to order.

❉ CROSS GRID JACQUARD PLUSH. 47% cotton, 53% wool. 50″ wide. No. 98657-11 (brown); 13 additional colors.

PONGEE

BRUNSCHWIG AND FILS

❉ PONGEE SILK. 100% silk. 50″ wide. No. 5300 (blanc cassé); No. 5303 (ivoire). Additional colors available.

DECORATORS WALK

❉ PONGEE. 100% silk. 45″ wide. No. HC63381 (off-white); No. HC63380 (natural).

❉ PONGEE. 100% silk. 50″ wide. No. T35771 (natural); No. T35770 (white).

FAR EASTERN FABRICS

Usually stocks 100% silk pongee in several widths. Write for current samples.

SCALAMANDRÉ

❉ PONGEE. 100% silk. 52″ wide. No. 98169-1 (oyster).

REP

LEE JOFA

❉ HIGHLAND RIB CLOTH. 90% wool, 10% nylon. 59″ wide. No. 795350–795360 (20 colors).

❉ LUCIEN REP. 96% wool, 4% other fiber. 51″ wide. No. 924300–924311 (6 colors).

SCALAMANDRÉ

❉ REGENT REP. 100% cotton. 52″ wide. No. 99754 series (22 colors).

❉ WOOL REP. 100% wool. 52″ wide. No. 99447 (7 colors).

SUNFLOWER STUDIO
❋ UPHOLSTERY SERGE. 100% wool. 36″ wide. Handwoven. No. X14.12 (cream white); can be dyed to order, 36 colors available.

SERGE

Plain and textured silks have never disappeared from production. Many excellent failles, moires, satins and taffetas are available from companies specializing in drapery fabrics. Brunschwig and Fils, Scalamandré and Schumacher have designated certain of their patterns as museum reproductions, primarily because of criteria relating to texture. In addition, Clarence House, Decorators Walk and other companies have excellent silks. The variety is tremendous, making careful selection of a prototype essential. When working with a limited budget, one might also want to consider certain synthetics or fiber blends that closely resemble silk.

SILKS

COWTAN AND TOUT
❋ CANDY STRIPE. Mid- to late 19th century. 100% cotton, glazed. 54″ wide. No. 88049-5 (blue on white ground); No. 88049-3 (red on white ground). Minimum order two yards.

STRIPES

ROSE CUMMING CHINTZES
❋ STRIPES. Mid- to late 19th century. 100% cotton, glazed. 50″ wide. Blue and white. No number; order by name only.

SCHUMACHER
COLONIAL WILLIAMSBURG REPRODUCTIONS
Documents at Colonial Williamsburg, Williamsburg, Va.
❋ RICHMOND STRIPE. Late 18th century, woven design. 72% mercerized cotton, 28% silk. 54″ wide, 2″ repeat. No. 20970 (document red).
❋ SHIR O SHAKKAR. 18th century, broad-striped seersucker. 100% cotton. 54″ wide. No. 81570 series (7 colors).
❋ WILLIAMSBURG STRIPE. 18th century. 100% cotton. 50″ wide. No. 132962 (red).
❋ WYTHE HOUSE STRIPE. Late 18th century. 100% cotton. 50″ wide. No. 111342 (document two reds).

DECORATORS WALK
❋ EMBROIDERED CURTAINS. 100% cotton. 4′ wide, 3 yards long. No. HC 77095 (ivory); No. HC77094 (white). Sold in pairs only.

**TAMBOUR
CURTAINS**

GREEFF FABRICS
This firm stocks a variety of tambour curtain designs that are suitable for late 19th-century work.

SCALAMANDRÉ
❋ MEISSONIER BORDER PANELS. 100% cotton batiste, embroidered. 53″ wide, 3 yards long. No. 96140-0 (white). Sold in pairs only.

MEISSONIER BORDER PANELS. Scalamandré. White.

TICKING

Closely woven cotton and linen fabrics used for bed ticking came in a variety of patterns, usually stripes. Modern blue-and-white striped bed ticking is little changed in appearance since the late 18th century. Waverly's "Cranston Plaid" (page 124) is a documentary reproduction of a factory-woven early 19th-century bed ticking in the textile collection at Old Sturbridge Village, Sturbridge, Mass. For those who wish to use handwoven ticking, one pattern of stripes is given in Grace Rogers Cooper's account *The Copp Family Textiles*. Ticking may also be ordered from:

SUNFLOWER STUDIO
❋ LINEN TICKING. 100% linen. 30″wide. No. E2.1 (blue and cream).

Most firms carry trimmings in stock. Usually suitable silk or wool tapes and basic kinds of fringes can be found in a wide range of colors. Custom work may be necessary to match an example of original trimming. Several firms will undertake this kind of work, notably Brunschwig and Fils, Clarence House, Old World Weavers and Scalamandré. (Scalamandré has specialized equipment and trained personnel in the United States to undertake this kind of work; however, they are in great demand so there may be considerable delay.) **TRIMMINGS**

Plain and figured velvets have scarcely changed. They are readily available in mohair, cotton, linen and silk from most drapery fabric manufacturers. Washable synthetic velvets are also available. They are sometimes an acceptable inexpensive substitute for silk velvet if the color and texture are similar. Velvets can be embossed in a wide variety of period designs (see Embossing). A few velvets have been designated museum reproductions: **VELVET**

SCALAMANDRÉ
❋ GRAND CANAL VELVET. Suitable for late 19th-century upholstery and drapery. 100% cotton. 54"wide. No. 98655 series (27 colors).

SCHUMACHER
COLONIAL WILLIAMSBURG REPRODUCTIONS
❋ WICKER VELVERETTE. English, mid-18th century ("Manchester Stuff"). 100% cotton. 54"wide, all-over repeat. No. 70217 (document green and brown).

STROHEIM AND ROMANN
❋ WINTERTHUR VELVET. 100% cotton. 54" wide. No. 40488– 40498 (11 colors).

The texture and finishing of woolen fabrics have changed considerably over the last 200 years. For restoration work focusing on the period before 1850, unless color simulation is the sole criterion, it is necessary to use documentary reproductions (such as those listed on pages 26–30) or handwoven wool fabrics using tightly spun yarns. **WOOLS**

SUNFLOWER STUDIO
This firm can supply several of the early types, including camlet, worsted, serge and shalloon. This firm also offers a wool called calamanco, which is soft and unglazed but resembles some handwoven wools of the period, although it is unlike the glazed fabric originally called calamanco.

APPENDIX

Many of these firms are wholesale houses whose products are available "to the trade only." This means that their fabrics are sold only through architects, interior designers and the decorating departments of fine retail and furniture stores. In some cases, the firms will sell goods directly to nonprofit institutions such as museums, historical societies, preservation agencies and state-owned historic properties. When requesting a specific fabric, begin by writing to the main office of a firm. It may choose to deal with clients directly or may refer them to a local agent. Arrangements for custom reproductions should always be made through the main office.

AMAZON VINEGAR AND PICKLING WORKS DRYGOODS. 2218 East 11th Street, Davenport, Iowa 52803

BAILEY AND GRIFFIN. 1406 Mermaid Lane, Philadelphia, Pa. 19118

BRUNSCHWIG AND FILS. 979 Third Avenue, New York, N.Y. 10022

CLARENCE HOUSE. 40 East 57th Street, New York, N.Y. 10022

COWTAN AND TOUT. 979 Third Avenue, New York, N.Y. 10022

DECORATORS WALK. 171 East 56th Street, New York, N.Y. 10022. Representing: Lee Behren Silks, The Henrose Company, Henry Cassen, Peter Schneiders' Sons and Company, J.H. Thorpe and Company

DORR MILL STORE. Guild, N.H. 03754

FAR EASTERN FABRICS. 171 Madison Avenue, New York, N.Y. 10016

FONTHILL. 979 Third Avenue, New York, N.Y. 10022

GREEFF FABRICS. 155 East 56th Street, New York, N.Y. 10022. Representing: E.C. Carter

HAMILTON-ADAMS. 104 West 40th Street, New York, N.Y. 10018

I.D. INTERNATIONAL. 979 Third Avenue, New York, N.Y. 10022

LEE JOFA. 979 Third Avenue, New York, N.Y. 10022

OLD WORLD WEAVERS. 136 East 55th Street, New York, N.Y. 10022

ROSE CUMMING CHINTZES. 232 East 59th Street, New York, N.Y. 10022

RUE DE FRANCE. 38 Bellevue Avenue, Suite 242, Newport, R.I. 02842

SCALAMANDRÉ. 950 Third Avenue, New York, N.Y. 10022

SCHUMACHER. 919 Third Avenue, New York, N.Y. 10022

STROHEIM AND ROMANN. 155 East 56th Street, New York, N.Y. 10022

SUNFLOWER STUDIO. 2851 Road B½, Grand Junction, Colo. 81501

THE TWIGS. 5700 Third Street, San Francisco, Calif. 94124

ULSTER WEAVING COMPANY. 148 Madison Avenue, New York, N.Y. 10018

WAVERLY FABRICS. 58 West 40th Street, New York, N.Y. 10018

SPECIALTY SOURCES

HANDWOVEN FABRICS

Weavers guilds in many cities and regions can provide information about persons who will undertake custom reproduction of handwoven fabrics. Several who have specialized in this area are:

NANCY BORDEN. 187 Marcy Street, Portsmouth, N.H. 03801

ALYCE HUNT, HIGH TIDE STUDIO. 49 Iris Street, Mahtomedi, Minn. 55115

CONSTANCE LA LENA, SUNFLOWER STUDIO. 2851 Road B½, Grand Junction, Colo. 81501 (illustrated catalog "Sampler of Early American Fabrics;" also with 24 handwoven swatches attached).

THE C.S. SMUCKERS. R.R. 1, State Route 287, West Liberty, Ohio 43357

LINEN UPHOLSTERY TAPE

ATTWILL FURNITURE COMPANY. 703 Washington Street, Lynn, Mass. 01901 (has available 18-yard rolls of 100% linen "English Webbing"). 100% linen girth web, available at many tack shops, is also good for this purpose.

NETTED BED CANOPIES AND EDGINGS

AUSTIN FARM HOUSE. P.O. Box 815, Richmond, Va. 23207

BIGGS. Direct Mail Department, 105 East Grace Street, Richmond, Va. 23219 (furniture catalog)

CARTER CANOPIES. Elsie M. Carter, P.O. Box 3372, 135 Grant Street, Eden, N.C. 27288-2022

COHASSET COLONIALS. Cohasset, Mass. 02025 (catalog)

LAURA COPENHAVER INDUSTRIES. Rosemont, Marion, Va. 24354 (catalog)

PATRICK DORMAN. 1705 Summit Avenue, No. 306, Seattle, Wash. 98122 (edgings only)

VIRGINIA GOODWIN. P.O. Box 36603, Charlotte, N.C. 28236

MRS. SHELDON HOWE. 176 Main Street, Northfield, Mass. 01360 (traditional Deerfield designs; custom orders only)

SHAKER CHAIR TAPE

COMMUNITY INDUSTRIES. Hancock Shaker Village, P.O. Box 898, Pittsfield, Mass. 01202. (Available in ¾" and ⅞" widths. 10 colors. Sample requests should be accompanied by a stamped, self-addressed

envelope. Taping instructions are included with each order.)
SHAKER WORKSHOPS. P.O. Box 1028, Concord, Mass. 01742. (Available in ⅝" and 1" widths. 12 colors in 5- and 10-yard rolls. Greater variety in color available to the trade. Catalog and tape samples.)

TOBACCO CLOTH

WILSON'S. Personal Shopper, 285 Main Street, Greenfield, Mass. 01301

TRIMMINGS

STANDARD TRIMMING CORPORATION. 1114 First Avenue, New York, N.Y. 10021

GLOSSARY

Identification of textiles referred to in early documents is complicated by the ways in which the meaning of the names has changed over time. Fabrics denoted by certain names have changed in texture and appearance or even in characteristic fiber content, making it important to understand the definition of the names at specific historical periods. In addition, subtle differences that were once commonly understood by manufacturers, merchants and consumers are now extremely difficult to discern. In some cases, several different names were used for the same type of goods, with the name denoting a place of manufacture rather than a distinctly different type of fabric. The best way to begin to determine the meaning of a specific name at a particular period is to consult a contemporary dictionary, encyclopedia or merchant's guide. In addition to works of a broad general interest, the following specialized publications are particularly helpful:

Beck, S. William. *The Draper's Dictionary, A Manual of Textile Fabrics: Their History and Applications.* London, 1882.

Cole, George S. *A Complete Dictionary of Dry Goods.* Rev. ed. New York: Textile Publishing Company, 1892.

Dickinson, William, ed. *A General Commercial Dictionary Comprehending Trade, Manufactures and Navigation, Also Agriculture as Far as It Is Connected with Commerce.* 2d ed. London, 1819.

BAIZE. Coarsely woven woolen cloth in a tabby weave, finished with a long nap. Used in the 18th and 19th centuries as a protective cover for carpets, tables and bookcases and as aprons in clothes presses, as well as for clothing, especially the lining of cloaks and coats. Not particularly successful as a writing surface unless glued down but sometimes used in this way despite its soft texture. Green appears to have been the most common color, although blue and red were also used.

BATISTE. Fine lightweight cotton or bleached white linen, usually cotton.

BLOTCH. In printed textiles, background color applied with the areas intended for the design reserved (left white) to heighten the color contrast.

BOBBINET. Machine-woven or "imitation" cotton lace, having a nearly hexagonal mesh. The foundation of machine-made lace. First successfully made in 1809 by John Heathcoat in England. Also refers to curtains with machine-woven insertion and edgings appliqued to a machine-made net ground cloth.

BOCKING. Coarse wool flannel or baize cloth, named for its place of origin, a city in Essex, England, well known in the 18th and 19th centuries for the manufacture of this type of cloth.

BOURETTE. A slubby silk usually spun from flawed cocoons; can be twill or plain weave.

BROADCLOTH. Firm tabby woven wool, fulled tightly, napped and shorn to a smooth, velvety surface.

BROCADE. A figured fabric in which the design is woven in additional contrasting color wefts restricted to the area of the design and not extended from selvage to selvage; these threads appear on the surface only in the areas required by the design. The background fabric can be tabby, twill or satin weave. The designs are frequently flowers or sprays of foliage.

BROCATELLE. A special form of lampas with a pattern in one weave on a ground of a contrasting texture, sometimes a satin weave. Often, heavy linen is used for extra ground wefts, which contrast with the silk pattern wefts but do not appear on the surface of the fabric. The cloth is woven tightly, thus sometimes causing the design elements to appear puffy; it can be made flat by adjusting the weaving tensions for the different fibers. In the last quarter of the 19th century, inexpensive brocatelles were made of silk and cotton or of cotton alone and used for curtains, upholstery and carriage linings.

BRUSSELS CURTAINS. Finely embroidered designs on fine-gauge cotton net. The enclosed surfaces of the design motifs are filled in with embroidery of still finer threads. The finest Brussels curtains were known as duchesse curtains at the end of the 19th century.

CALAMANCO. A glazed worsted fabric in a satin weave, either solid color or woven with figured designs in colors resembling silk brocades. See Hazel E. Cummin, "Calamanco," in *Antiques,* April 1941, p. 184.

CALENDER. A cloth-finishing machine using two or more heated cylinders through which the fabric is passed. Calendering gives a smooth, even surface to the fabric. If one cylinder rotates faster than the other, one side of the fabric will have a shiny, or glazed, surface. If one cylinder has a pattern raised on it, the surface will be embossed with the pattern; this may be an overall watered, or moired, design or a specific motif such as flowers and ribbons or Gothic arches. This technique is especially suitable for embellishing moreens and velvets.

CALICO. Cotton cloth with patterns printed in one or more colors. In the 18th and early 19th centuries, calico referred to the printed cloth imported from India and sometimes to any plain-woven cotton — woven, printed, checked or striped. Now usually refers to cotton prints with small, stylized patterns.

CAMBRIC. Originally, fine bleached linen; later, a fine cotton of plain weave with a highly glazed surface. Cheaper cotton cambric of a very loose weave is used for underupholstery on seat furniture.

CAMLET. Unglazed worsted fabric of a plain weave. Descriptive of a group of 18th-century materials including harrateen and china (cheyney). See Hazel E. Cummin, "Camlet," in *Antiques,* December 1942, pp. 309–12.

CHEYNEY. A plain worsted fabric whose name is apparently derived from a phonetic spelling of a colloquial pronunciation of "China."

CHINTZ. Glazed cotton cloth of plain weave. In the 18th century, always printed. First manufactured in India; then imitated elsewhere. Printed designs usually have at least five colors and are frequently large-scale floral patterns. Now also refers to solid-colored, glazed cottons with a fine thread count.

CLOTH. In 18th-century sources, usually denotes finely spun and woven woolen broadcloth.

COLORWAY. One color combination of a style or pattern.

CRETONNE. A stout cotton cloth, usually unglazed, printed on one or both sides. Popular in the last half of the 19th century for window curtains, sofa covers and chair coverings. At the present time it is unavailable in the United States.

DAMASK. A fabric with reversible, solid-colored, woven designs on contrasting glossy and dull fabric surfaces; can be woven of any fiber or combination of fibers, most commonly silk or linen.

DARNIX (also Dornick). Heavy linen cloth; usually refers to checked or damask woven table linen.

DIAPER. Fabric containing motifs of small woven patterns in linen or cotton white goods, typically diamonds, bird's eyes, arrowheads or chevrons.

DIMITY. Cotton cloth with woven ribs forming a pattern of either stripes or checks. The type of dimity used as a furnishing fabric was considerably heavier than that introduced about 1825 and still popular for clothing and window curtains. This lighter type of dimity became popular in the early 20th century for window curtains. In the late 19th century dimity was sometimes printed with small-figured designs, but it is usually white. For more detail, see Hazel E. Cummin, "What Was Dimity in 1790?," *Antiques*, July 1940, pp. 23–25.

DISCHARGE PRINTING. A technique that produces a pattern on a ground of a solid color. The cloth is first piece dyed and then block printed with a chemical discharging agent, which removes the color from the areas of the design, leaving a solid background.

DOCUMENT. A historic fabric or fabric design, the source of color and design for a reproduction.

DOCUMENTARY COLORWAY. A modern manufacturers' term used to indicate that the colors of a reproduction fabric are those of the original document.

DOUBLE NET CURTAINS. Curtains made with one layer of fine-gauge, machine-made net embroidered on another, the ground of the upper layer then being entirely cut away, leaving the net doubled only in the area of the designs. In many cases, hand embroidery was used for additional embellishment.

DOUBLE WOVEN. Two ply, or made with two layers interwoven at regular intervals.

DROP REPEAT. A large-scale design that can be matched lengthwise only by alternating motifs in a zigzag pattern across two widths; requires extra yardage.

DURANT. A glazed woolen fabric, better quality than tammy. Folded lengthwise during calendering, therefore having a characteristic sharp center crease.

ELL. A long measure, mainly for cloth, of different length in different countries. An English ell equals 45 inches, or 1¼ yards.

FAILLE. A fabric having horizontal ribs formed by the use of weft yarns heavier than warp yarns; not as heavy as a rep. Until the 20th century, usually used for clothing rather than upholstery or drapery.

FANCY GROUND. In printed textiles, a style especially popular in the second quarter of the 19th century in which the background areas are printed with finely engraved small dots, chevrons, wandering lines or other simple motifs.

FELT. Woolen cloth made without weaving, a matted layer of randomly arranged wool fibers.

FILLING. Threads woven from selvage to selvage, crosswise on the loom. Also called weft.

FUGITIVE COLORS. Those dyes that fade most rapidly as a result of exposure to sunlight or laundry solutions.

FURNITURE. A term commonly used in the 18th century to denote the full equipment of something. Hence, "bed and furniture" meant the mattress, bolster, pillows, sheets, pillow cases and sometimes the blankets and curtains; "tea table and furniture" referred to the table as well as its accompanying ceramic and metal objects for the service of tea. In the case of "window curtain and furniture," the furniture referred to the rods, hooks, rings and pulleys, as well as the cloth.

FURNITURE CHECK. A kind of checked linen or cotton used from the 17th century to the present for loose cases or slipcovers, window curtains, bed hangings and underupholstery on seating furniture. Checks of various sizes were used for this purpose, but they were usually in units of at least one-half inch. Note that 18th-century references to "furniture" do not necessarily specify check.

FUSTIAN. In the 18th century, refers to any of a wide variety of linen-and-cotton or occasionally all-cotton textiles, which can be herringbone, ribbed, diaper or plain-woven. In the early 19th century, fustians were commonly ribbed on one side; in the 18th century, they were most commonly used for work clothing.

GALLOON. Originally a narrow worsted tape or binding. By the end of the 19th century, it was made of wool, silk, cotton, gold or silver threads.

GAUFRAGE. An embossing technique in which a heated metal cylinder with a raised design on it is pressed against the pile of a plain fabric, such as plush or velvet, thereby transferring the pattern.

GAUZE. Plain-woven fabric having an openwork effect. Used for mosquito pavilions or bed canopies, especially in the southern colonies and West Indies. Also used for covering paintings, looking glasses and chandeliers in the summer season.

GIMP. A flat trimming made by twisting silk, worsted or cotton threads around a foundation thread or wire and then worked in an open design; frequently used for valance and curtain edging as well as for furniture trimming. Often used in colors that contrast brightly with those of the fabric to which the gimp is attached.

GLAZED. Having a smooth and lustrous surface on the exposed, or right, side only.

HARRATEEN. In 18th-century England and colonial America, a wool moire, sometimes embossed.

HERRINGBONE. A twill weave in which a stripe of short diagonal lines is juxtaposed to another in which the short lines go in the opposite direction, thus forming an overall zigzag effect.

HOLLAND. An 18th- and early 19th-century term for closely woven linens, first manufactured in Holland but later made throughout Europe and the British Isles. In the mid- and late 19th century, the term also referred to starched cotton cloth that was heavily glazed; it was used most commonly for window shades. "Brown holland" refers to unbleached linen.

HORSEHAIR FABRIC (also Hair Cloth). Fabric woven of horse mane and tail hairs with a cotton, linen or worsted warp. Used for sofa upholstery and chair seats; can be tabby, satin or pattern woven. Eighteenth-century examples have a linen warp and ribbed tabby weave structure. Nineteenth-century examples are more commonly satin weave; some complex brocade designs are also from this later period. Black horsehair fabric is made with dyed black and gray hairs, while the lighter colored hairs are dyed green, claret, crimson or, less frequently, blue or gold.

IRISH POINT LACE CURTAINS. Cotton net panels with applique designs; the areas between the designs are cut away and the opening bound with embroidery and crossed by cords or threads sometimes fastened together in designs called spiders.

JACQUARD. A selective shedding device added to looms. Developed in France by M. Jacquard, who received a medal for it in Paris in 1801 and continued to refine the system, perfecting it in 1803; first brought to America in 1823. Originally used extensively for silk weaving but soon also for carpets, coverlets, table linens and all other types of textiles. Produces complex woven figures through the use of a series of punch cards. Still used today.

LAMPAS. A figured fabric of satin weave using additional wefts and warps to form a design in one texture on the ground of another; the additional threads are woven into the back of the fabric. The ground may be tabby, twill, satin or damask. The design effect is that of a two-color damask, but the fabric is not reversible.

LINSEY-WOOLSEY. A coarse flannel with a linen warp and woolen weft. Usually homespun and handwoven. Less common in colonial America than recent romantic history would suggest.

MARSEILLES. A heavy, corded cotton fabric with a pattern woven in the goods; usually white, it resembled hand quilting. Used primarily for bed coverings from the late 18th to the early 20th century; also used for petticoats and vesting in the mid-19th century.

MATELASSÉ. A double-woven cloth that simulates quilting by interlocking in some areas to produce a puckered effect.

MERCERIZE. A treatment of cotton with caustic soda to increase strength, enhance receptiveness to dyes and impart a characteristic shine. Developed in 1866 by John Mercer, an English calico printer.

MESH. In bobbinet or netting, one hole; in lace, the entire background.

MOIRE. Clouded or watered effects on ribbed wool or silk fabrics, achieved by the application of intense but uneven pressure to the dampened fabric.

MOREEN. In the 18th century, a stout worsted or mohair fabric; by the late 19th century, often wool with a cotton warp. Sometimes plain but more often embossed with a design of fancy flowers or other elaborate figures, sometimes with a watered background in imitation of moire. Used extensively for upholstery and heavy curtains for beds and windows.

MOSQUITO NETTING. Commercial types made in the late 19th century included a coarse cotton gauze with large open mesh, usually having each warp thread confined between two weft strands. Earlier, bobbinet and gauze were used for this purpose.

MULL. A thin, almost transparent, soft cotton muslin; often used for clothing.

MULTI. A manufacturers' term for a fabric containing many colors.

MUSLIN. A fine thin cotton cloth with a downy nap on its surface. Generally plain but sometimes decorated with openwork or embroidery. In recent years, somewhat more coarse in texture.

NAIL. In English cloth measure, 2.25 inches, or $1/16$ yard. Appears as the abbreviation "N" in sewing instructions.

NAP. The surface fibers of felt and woven cloth; may be raised by brushing.

NATURAL FIBERS. Animal or vegetable fibers used for textiles; most commonly, cotton, wool, silk or linen.

NET. An open textile fabric of any fiber, tied or woven with a mesh of any size. Nets are formed by threads being wound around each other and knotted. Made by hand until the invention of the bobbinet machine in 1809. The term "net" is also used for light, woven fabrics, such as gauze.

NOTTINGHAM LACE CURTAINS. Panels of machine-made lace with integral designs; so called because they are made on a lace curtain machine invented in Nottingham, England, which was also the principal place of their manufacture during the last half of the 19th century. This fabric has always been available in various designs and qualities.

OSNABURG. A kind of coarse linen, plain woven, originally made in Osnabrück, Germany, but later imitated in England and elsewhere. Sometimes spelled "Ozenbriggs." By the second half of the 19th century, the name referred to coarse cottons, often unbleached.

PALAMPORE. A cotton bed covering from India, usually printed or painted with large-scale, highly naturalistic designs, often a tree of life.

PASSEMENTERIE. Edgings or trimmings, especially those made out of gimp, braid or cords; may be silk, cotton, wool or metallic threads.

PATCH. Printed cottons, usually chintz furnishing fabrics. A term frequently encountered in New England manuscripts and printed documents, c. 1750–1850. After 1840, fabrics printed with trompe l'oeil patchworks were also called patch.

PIECE DYED. Cloth dyed, after weaving, "in the piece," in contrast to cloth woven of colored yarns or printed on one surface only.

PILE. Regular, close nap made of threads standing at right angles to the web. Usually sheared to form a smooth and even surface. The textured furry surface of velvet or plush.

PLUSH. A fabric with an even pile, longer and less dense than that of velvet. Used for upholstery in the mid- to late 19th century. May be silk, mohair or wool. Can be embellished with woven patterns or embossed designs.

PLY. The number of strands of which a yarn is made. Also, a thickness or layer of cloth.

PONGEE. Thin, soft, uncolored natural, or raw, silk.

PORTIERE. A heavy curtain hung at a doorway to prevent drafts, to provide privacy or to enhance the decorative effect of an interior scheme. Usually hung on large rings that slide on a pole placed above the doorway.

QUALITY BINDING. Wide worsted tape, used for carpet binding. Often referred to in 19th-century documents simply as "quality."

QUARTER. A measurement of a quarter yard (nine inches). A 12-4 (twelve-quarter) lace curtain is three yards long; a 14-4 carpet is three and one-half yards wide.

QUILTING. In the 18th century, can refer to tufting in upholstery of chairs or cushions. Normally, however, a bed cover made of two layers of fabric having wadding or batting between them and stitched together in geometric or fancy patterns.

REP. Fabric with closely woven, crosswise ribs. Wool or worsted rep in solid colors was popular from about 1835 for upholstery and heavy curtains. In the late 19th century "furniture rep," a flowered cotton in a thin weave, was also manufactured. Silk reps were usually but not always used for clothing.

REPEAT. One complete pattern motif.

RESIST DYE. An 18th-century method of indigo printing in which a resist paste inhibited the dye. See Montgomery, *Printed Textiles*, pp. 194–211.

ROLLER PRINTING. Textile printing done with engraved metal cylinders, a technique first developed in 1783 and perfected in the early 19th century. Each color element of a design requires a separate cylinder and is printed directly on the cloth. Sometimes referred to as cylinder printing or machine printing.

RUSSELL. Ribbed or corded fabric, usually a worsted satin.

RUSSIA LEATHER. In the early 18th century, seal or goatskin dyed black, imported from Russia for upholstery; later widely imitated.

SATEEN. A smooth, satin-weave cloth usually made of mercerized cotton. Used for window hangings, bed coverings and occasionally as a ground for embroidery in the last half of the 19th and early 20th centuries.

SATIN. A fabric that is shiny on one side and dull on the other, created by a special weave leaving numerous warp floats on the surface. Usually silk; also wool and linen.

SCRIM. Loosely woven cotton, sometimes with a heavy weave, used in the late 19th century for window curtains and drapery.

SELVAGE. The lengthwise edges of a piece of cloth, often of a different color and heavier threads, sometimes even a different weave. Intended to prevent raveling. Also called list.

SERGE. A strong, twill-woven wool fabric with a pronounced diagonal rib, made in various qualities. After leather and turkeywork, the third most popular chair covering in late 17th- and early 18th-century America.

SHALLOON. A lightweight twilled wool or worsted fabric.

SHEERS. Thin, pliable, translucent cotton or linen textiles. Since about 1810, these types of fabric have been used for undercurtains; today the curtains themselves are called sheers.

SLUBS. Lumps on thread, formed by careless spinning. Deliberate use of slubs to give an antique effect to finished cloth is inappropriate for restoration purposes.

STORMONT. A textile pattern introduced in the factory of Sir Robert Peel in the 1780s. The design is characterized by a background of dots of color. At first these were sprayed from a broom; later, brushes were used. Eventually the dots were produced by metal teeth in a wooden roller.

STUFF. Any woven woolen cloth without nap, usually a worsted.

TABBINET. A silk and wool fabric with a watered surface, used for upholstery. A superior type was called tabaret; it was characterized by alternating stripes of watered and satin surfaces in different colors.

TABBY. A plain-weave structure in which one warp passes over and then under a single weft thread. The warp and weft threads are of the same size and are set with the same number per inch, thereby giving a balanced weave. Also, a fabric woven in this way.

TAFFETA. A closely woven, firm fabric of even weight and tension, known by its glossy surface. Usually silk but can be linen. There is no difference between the two sides.

TAMBOUR. Embroidery worked on fine cotton cloth using a small hook on the upper side and bringing threads up through the cloth to form a chain stitch on the upper surface. Worked on yard goods in India to this day. Machine-embroidered curtain panels have been made in this stitch since the mid-19th century. The center of their manufacture continues to be Switzerland.

TAMMY. A loosely woven wool of medium quality.

TASSEL. A pendant ornament. Before the 20th century, usually a wooden mold covered with strands of wool or silk. Now often merely a cluster of threads or cords, gathered together at the top.

TOBACCO CLOTH. Unbleached white cotton cloth used for protecting certain tobacco plants from direct sunlight during the growing process, thus producing shadegrown tobacco. Resembles the texture and weight of pure cotton muslin.

TOILE. From "toile imprimée," meaning "printed cotton." Now, generally refers to copperplate-printed fabrics or to those printed in the style of the 18th-century copperplate designs on either cotton or linen cloth; more correctly, those of French origin.

TURKEY RED. Bright red calico dyed with madder fixed by the use of oil; a very durable color. This technique was a specialty of Alsatian calico printers, who kept it a closely guarded secret.

TURKEYWORK. An upholstery fabric having a knotted wool pile in bright colors with a black background. Made as covers for chairs, settees and stools. It is believed that in many cases furniture was made specifically to fit the finished covers. Used from the late 17th century to the mid-18th century. Not currently available as a commercial reproduction.

TWILL. A weave in which the weft threads pass over one and then under two warp threads, thus producing a diagonal pattern.

VELVET. A pile fabric produced by the use of an extra series of warps passing over wires in loops. It can be plain (left as woven), or the loops can be cut when the wires are removed. If a pattern is created by alternating areas of cut and uncut loops, the fabric is called ciselé velvet. If the pattern is woven leaving some areas without pile, it is called voided velvet. Usually wool, silk or cotton.

VERMICELLI, VERMICULAR. A design motif consisting of an endless meandering line. Referred to in at least one 18th-century document as "worm."

WARP. The threads stretched lengthwise on the loom, usually spun more tightly than the weft and therefore stronger.

WEFT. The threads interwoven with the warp, running crosswise in the goods, from selvage to selvage. Also called filling.

WELTING. In the 18th century, the term for piping in upholstery. Then made of straight strips of fabric sewn over tightly spun linen cord. Used to strengthen seams in furniture upholstery.

WORSTED. Fabric made of long staple wool that has been combed to make the fibers lie parallel to each other when spun. The effect is silky and durable.

This listing emphasizes books and articles that are likely to be available in public library collections and through interlibrary loan services. Some are inexpensive reprints of 19th-century sources. The books cited here that will be most difficult to find are the expensive catalog of the textile collections of the Victoria and Albert Museum and the Musée de l'Impression sur Etoffes; these contain lavish color illustrations that will certainly be useful.

Adrosko, Rita. *Natural Dyes and Home Dyeing.* New York: Dover, 1971.

Ayres, James. *The Shell Book of the Home in Britain.* London: Faber and Faber, 1981.

Baumgarten, Linda. "The Textile Trade in Boston, 1650–1700." In *Arts of the Anglo-American Community in the Seventeenth Century, Winterthur Conference Report 1974,* pp. 219–73. Charlottesville: University Press of Virginia, 1975.

Beecher, Catherine. *A Treatise on Domestic Economy.* 1841. Rpt. New York: Source Book Press, 1970.

Beecher, Catherine, and Stowe, Harriet Beecher. *The American Woman's Home.* 1869. Rpt. Hartford, Conn.: Stowe-Day Foundation, 1975.

Beer, Alice B. *Trade Goods: A Study of Indian Chintz.* Washington, D.C.: Smithsonian Institution Press, 1970.

Brightman, Anna. "Window Curtains in Colonial Boston and Salem," *Antiques,* August 1964, pp. 184–87.

————. *Window Treatments for Historic Houses, 1700–1850.* Preservation Leaflet Series, no. 14. Washington, D.C.: National Trust for Historic Preservation, 1968.

————. "Woolen Window Curtains: Luxury in Colonial Boston and Salem," *Antiques,* December, 1964, pp. 722–27.

British Textile Design in the Victoria and Albert Museum. Tokyo: Gakken, 1980. Vol. I, *The Middle Ages to Rococo* (1200–1750). Vol. II, *Rococo to Victorian* (1750–1850). Vol. III, *Victorian to Modern* (1850–1940).

Bronson, J.R. *The Domestic Manufacturer's Assistant.* Reissued as *Early American Weaving and Dyeing: The Domestic Manufacturer's Assistant and Family Directory in the Arts of Weaving and Dyeing.* New York: Dover, 1977.

Caulfeild, Sophia, and Saward, Blanche C. *The Dictionary of Needlework.* 1882. Facsimile eds. New York: Arno Press, 1972; Dover, 1972 (2 vols.).

Chefs d'Oeuvre du Musée de l'Impression sur Etoffes, Mulhouse. Tokyo: Gakken, 1978. Vol. I, *Imprimis Français I.* Vol. II, *Imprimis Français II, Européens et Orientaux.* Vol. III, *Dessins, Emprientes et Papiers Peints.*

Clark, Fiona. *William Morris Wallpapers and Chintzes.* New York: St. Martin's Press.

Clinton, Elizabeth. "Regency Furnishing Designs," *Connoisseur,* June 1978, pp. 106–17.

Clouzot, Henri, and Morris, Frances. *Painted and Printed Fabrics.* New

York: Metropolitan Museum of Art, 1927.

Cooper, Grace Rogers. *The Copp Family Textiles.* Washington, D.C.: Smithsonian Institution Press, 1971.

Cooper, Nicholas. *The Opulent Eye: Late Victorian and Edwardian Taste in Interior Design.* London: Architectural Press, 1976.

Cornforth, John. *English Interiors 1790–1848.* London: Barrie and Jenkins, 1978.

Cummings, Abbott Lowell, ed. *Bed Hangings: A Treatise on Fabrics and Styles in the Curtaining of Beds, 1650–1850.* Boston: Society for the Preservation of New England Antiquities, 1961.

————. *Rural Household Inventories.* Boston: Society for the Preservation of New England Antiquities, 1964.

D'Allemagne, Henry-Rene. *La Toile Imprimée et les Indiennes de Traite.* 2 vols. Paris: Gruend, 1942.

Des Dorelotiers aux Passementiers. Paris: Musée des Arts Décoratifs, 1973.

DeWolfe, Elsie. *The House in Good Taste.* New York: Century, 1913.

Dornsife, Samuel J. "Design Sources for Nineteenth-Century Window Hangings." In *Winterthur Portfolio,* 10. Charlottesville: University Press of Virginia, 1975.

Downing, A. J. *The Architecture of Country Houses, with Remarks on Interiors, Furniture.* 1850. Rpt. New York: Dover, 1969.

Eastlake, Charles L. *Hints on Household Taste.* 4th ed. 1878. Rpt. New York: Dover, 1969.

Edwards, Ralph, and Ramsey, L. G. G. *Connoisseur Period Guides to the Houses, Decorations, Furnishing and Chattels of the Classic Periods.* 6 vols. New York: Reynal, 1957–58; Bonanza, 1968 (6 vols. in 1).

————. *Etoffes Imprimées Françaises, Musée de l'Impression sur Etoffes de Mulhouse.* Catalog of an exhibition held at Kyoto, Japan, 1981.

Fairclough, Oliver, and Learly, Emmeline. *Textiles by William Morris and Morris and Company 1861–1940.* London: Thames and Hudson, 1981.

Fales, Martha Gandy. "A Nineteenth-Century Guide to Making Curtains." *Antiques,* March 1981, pp. 682–85.

Floud, Peter, and Morris, Barbara. Series of articles on chintz design. *Antiques,* March–December 1957.

Fowler, John, and Cornforth, John. *English Decoration in the 18th Century.* Princeton, N.J.: Pyne Press, 1974.

Gallagher, Constance Dann. *Linen Heirlooms.* Newton Centre, Mass.: Charles T. Branford Company, 1968.

————. *More Linen Heirlooms.* Boston: The Weavers Guild, 1982.

Garrett, Elisabeth Donaghy. "The American Home, Part I: 'Centre and Circumfrence': The American Domestic Scene in the Age of the Enlightenment." *Antiques,* January 1983, pp. 214–25; "Part II: Lighting Devices and Practices," *Antiques,* February 1983, pp. 408–17; "Part III: The Bedchamber," *Antiques,* March 1983, pp. 612–25.

Harrison, Constance Cary. *Woman's Handiwork in Modern Houses*. New York: Scribner's, 1881.

Irwin, John, and Brett, Katherine. *The Origins of Chintz*. London: Her Majesty's Stationery Office, 1970.

Jobe, Brock. "The Boston Furniture Industry." In *Boston Furniture of the Eighteenth Century*. Boston: The Colonial Society of Massachusetts, 1974.

The Lady's Handbook of Fancy Needlework. London: 1880. Facsimile ed. *Late Victorian Needlework for Victorian Houses*. Watkins Glen, N.Y.: American Life Foundation, 1979.

Lasdun, Susan. *Victorians at Home*. New York: Viking, 1981.

Le Musée de l'Impression sur Etoffes de Mulhouse. Mulhouse: Société Industrielle de Mulhouse, 1975.

Little, Francis. *Early American Textiles*. New York: Century, 1931.

Loudon, J.C. *An Encyclopaedia of Cottage, Farm and Villa Architecture and Furniture*. London: Longman, Brown, Green and Longmans, 1842.

Lubell, Cecil. *Textile Collections of the World*. Cincinnati: Van Nostrand Reinhold Company, 1976–77. Vol. I, *United States and Canada*. Vol. II, *United Kingdom and Ireland*. Vol. III, *France*.

Mayhew, Edgar deN., and Myers, Minor, Jr. *A Documentary History of American Interiors*. New York: Scribner's, 1980.

Merrell, Jeannette. "Chintzes from Portugal," *Antiques*, June 1928, pp. 496–98.

Michie, Audrey. "Charleston Textile Imports, 1738–1742," *Journal of Early Southern Decorative Arts*, May 1981, pp. 21–39.

Montgomery, Florence. "Antique and Reproduction Furnishing Fabrics in Historic Houses and Period Rooms," *Antiques*, January 1975, pp. 164–69.

––––––. "Eighteenth-Century English and American Furnishing Fashions," *Antiques*, February 1970, pp. 267–71.

––––––. "Furnishing Textiles at the John Brown House, Providence, Rhode Island," *Antiques*, March 1972, pp. 496–500.

––––––. "John Holker's Mid-Eighteenth Century 'Livre d' Enchantillons.'" In *Studies in Textile History*, edited by Veronika Gervers. Toronto: Royal Ontario Museum, 1977, pp. 214–31.

––––––. *Printed Textiles: English and American Cottons and Linens, 1700–1850*. New York: Viking, 1970.

––––––. "Room Furnishings as Seen in British Prints from the Lewis Walpole Library," *Antiques*. Part I, "Bed Hangings," June 1973, pp. 1068–75. Part II, "Window Curtains, Upholstery and Slip Covers," March 1974, pp. 522–33.

––––––. "Upholstery and Furnishing Fabrics." In *American Furniture, The Federal Period*, edited by Charles F. Montgomery. New York: Viking, 1966.

Morland, Frank A. *Practical Decorative Upholstery: Containing Full In-*

structions for Cutting, Making, and Hanging All Kinds of Interior Up-holstery Decoration. Boston and New York: 1890. Rpt. Edited by Martha Gandy Fales. New York: E. P. Dutton, 1979.

Nylander, Jane C. "Window Hangings," *Early American Life,* December 1979, pp. 40–43, 69.

————. *Beds and Bed Hangings.* Slide tape. Nashville: American Association for State and Local History, 1982.

Nylander, Jane C., and Sloat, Caroline Fuller. "White Curtains," *Early American Life,* August 1982, pp. 54–57.

Nylander, Richard C. "Documenting the Interior of Codman House: The Last Two Generations," *Old Time New England,* 1981, pp. 84–102.

Parkes, Frances Byerly. *Domestic Duties.* London: Longman, Hurst, Rees, Brown and Green, 1825.

Parry, Linda. *William Morris Textiles.* New York: Viking, 1983.

Peterson, Harold L. *Americans at Home.* New York: Scribner's, 1971. Reissued as *American Interiors from Colonial Times to the Late Victorians.* New York: Scribner's, 1979.

Pettit, Florence H. *America's Printed and Painted Fabrics, 1600–1900.* New York: Hastings House, 1970.

Praz, Mario. *An Illustrated History of Furnishing from the Renaissance to the Twentieth Century.* New York: Braziller, 1964. Reissued as *An Illustrated History of Interior Decorating from Pompeii to Art Nouveau.* New York: Thames and Hudson, 1982.

————. *Conversation Pieces.* University Park, Pa.: Pennsylvania State University, 1971.

Robinson, Stuart. *A History of Printed Textiles.* Cambridge, Mass.: MIT Press, 1969.

Rothstein, Natalie. "Silks Imported into America in the 18th Century, An Historical Survey." In *Irene Emery Roundtable on Museum Textiles, 1975 Proceedings: Imported and Domestic Textiles in Eighteenth-Century America.* Washington, D.C.: Textile Museum, 1976.

Rowe, Anne Pollard. "Crewel Embroidered Bed Hangings in Old and New England," *Bulletin of the Museum of Fine Arts, Boston,* 71 (1973), 365 and 366.

Schoelwer, Susan Prendergast. "Form, Function, and Meaning in the Use of Fabric Furnishings: A Philadelphia Case Study, 1700–1775," *Winterthur Portfolio,* Spring 1979, pp. 25–40.

Seale, William. *Recreating the Historic House Interior.* Nashville: American Association for State and Local History, 1979.

————. *The Tasteful Interlude: American Interiors Through the Camera's Eye, 1860–1917.* Rpt. Nashville: American Association for State and Local History, 1980.

Storey, Joyce. *The Thames and Hudson Manual of Dyes and Fabrics.* London: Thames and Hudson, 1978.

Talbot, George. *At Home: Domestic Life in the Post Centennial Era.*

Madison: State Historical Society of Wisconsin, 1976.

Thornton, Peter. *Baroque and Rococo Silks*. New York: Taplinger, 1965.

————. *Seventeenth-Century Interior Decoration in England, France and Holland*. New Haven: Yale University Press, 1978.

Toiles de Nantes, des XVIIIe et XIXe Siecles. Mulhouse: Musée de l'Impression sur Etoffes, 1977.

Victoria and Albert Museum. *English Printed Textiles: Large Picture Book No. 13*. London: Her Majesty's Stationery Office, 1960.

————. *Catalogue of a Loan Exhibition of English Chintz*. London: Author, 1960.

Webster, Thomas, and Parkes, Frances B. *Encyclopaedia of Domestic Economy*. New York: Harper, 1845.

Wharton, Edith, and Codman, Ogden, Jr. *The Decoration of Houses*. New York: Scribner's, 1897. Rpt. New York: W. W. Norton, 1978.

Wheeler, Candace. *The Development of Embroidery in America*. New York: Harper and Brothers, 1921.

————. *Principles of Home Decoration*. New York: Doubleday, Page and Company, 1908.

Williams, Henry T., and Jones, Mrs. C. S. *Beautiful Homes*. New York: Williams, 1878.

SOURCES OF
INFORMATION

AMERICAN SOCIETY OF INTERIOR DESIGNERS. 1430 Broadway, New York, N.Y. 10018

BOSCOBEL RESTORATION, INC. RFD 2, Garrison-on-Hudson, N.Y. 10028

COLONIAL WILLIAMSBURG FOUNDATION. P.O. Box C, Williamsburg, Va. 23187

COOPER-HEWITT MUSEUM. Smithsonian Institution, 2 East 91st Street, New York, N.Y. 10028

THE DECORATIVE ARTS TRUST. P.O. Box 1226, Camden, S.C. 29020

HISTORIC CHARLESTON FOUNDATION. 51 Meeting Street, Charleston, S.C. 29401

HISTORIC HOUSE ASSOCIATION OF AMERICA. 1600 H Street, N.W., Washington, D.C. 20006

HISTORIC SAVANNAH FOUNDATION. P.O. Box 1733, Savannah, Ga. 31402

METROPOLITAN MUSEUM OF ART. 82nd Street and Fifth Avenue, New York, N.Y. 10028

MUSÉE DES ARTS DÉCORATIFS. Palais du Louvre, Pavillon de Marsan, 107 rue de Rivoli, Paris, France 75000

MUSEUM OF EARLY SOUTHERN DECORATIVE ARTS. Drawer F, Salem Station, Winston-Salem, N.C. 27108

OLD ECONOMY VILLAGE. Harmonie Associates, Inc., 14th and Church Streets, Ambridge, Pa. 15003

OLD STURBRIDGE VILLAGE. Route 20, Sturbridge, Mass. 01566

SOCIETY FOR THE PRESERVATION OF NEW ENGLAND ANTIQUITIES. 141 Cambridge Street, Boston, Mass. 02114

VICTORIA AND ALBERT MUSEUM. Exhibition and Cromwell Roads, London SW 1, England

THE VICTORIAN SOCIETY IN AMERICA. 219 East Sixth Street, Philadelphia, Pa. 19106

WILLIAM MORRIS SOCIETY. 420 Riverside Drive, 7D, New York, N.Y. 10025

WINTERTHUR MUSEUM AND GARDENS. Route 52, Kennett Pike, Winterthur, Del. 19735

Fabrics for Historic Buildings was edited by Gretchen Smith, associate editor, The Preservation Press. Christine Klimonda assisted in the production.

The book was designed by Robert Wiser and Marc Meadows, Marc Meadows and Associates, Washington, D.C. It was composed in Cloister Old Style by General Typographers, Inc., Washington, D.C., and printed on 80# Mead Moistrite Matte by Wolk Press, Woodlawn, Md.

Photographs of patterns have been supplied by the manufacturers, except for those noted here: *Page 9*—Photograph by Barnaby Evans. Used with permission of the Rhode Island Historical Society. *Page 84* — Photograph by Henry E. Peach, Old Sturbridge Village, Sturbridge, Mass.

ACKNOWLEDG-
MENTS